BEIRUT

CITY OF REGRETS

PHOTOGRAPHS BY ELI REED

TEXT BY FOUAD AJAMI

BEIRUT
CITY OF REGRETS

W. W. NORTON & COMPANY

NEW YORK   LONDON

Published simultaneously in Canada by Penguin Books Canada Ltd.,
2801 John Street, Markham, Ontario L3R 1B4.

Printed in Italy.

The text of this book is composed in Gill Sans.
The composition is by Trufont Typographers
manufacturing is by American Pizzi Offset Corporation,
and the book was designed by Homans Design, Inc.

First Edition

Library of Congress Cataloging-in-Publication Data

Ajami, Fouad.
   Beirut : the city of regrets.

   1. Beirut (Lebanon)   2. Beirut (Lebanon)—History—
Pictorial works.   3. Lebanon—History—1975–
4. Lebanon—History—1975–   —Pictorial works.
I. Reed, Eli.   II. Title.
DS89.B4A54   1988   956.2   87-23987
ISBN 0-393-02490-3
ISBN 0-393-30507-4 pbk.

W. W. Norton & Company, Inc., 500 Fifth Avenue, New York, N.Y. 10110

W. W. Norton & Company Ltd., 37 Great Russell Street, London WC1B 3NU

1 2 3 4 5 6 7 8 9 0

Contents

Dedication   6

Acknowledgments   7

B E I R U T : City of Regrets   *Fouad Ajami*   9

Plates   *Eli Reed*   49

Photographers Notes   *Eli Reed*   177

End Notes   180

Source Notes   183

To Michelle Saltmarsh

—F.A.

To Terry and company for all the obvious reasons
and to Donald and L.G. for all the right ones.

—E.R.

Acknowledgments   Linda Healey, James L. Mairs, and William F. Rusin at W. W. Norton saw the possibility of this enterprise and saw it through. It was they who wanted the story of Beirut depicted and told, and who brought author and photographer together. In Beirut, the help of Dr. Farid el Khazen and Mr. Salem Chalabi came when it was needed. And also Kamel Cabbabe, Madame Eliane Zebara, Alexandra Moukalzel and her staff, Ali Hamdam, Francoise Demulder, Bill Kuykendal, and Rose Marie Wheeler provided invaluable assistance.

When political catastrophe came to Beirut there was plenty of material for the obituaries of the city. It was a pretentious city by the Mediterranean, it was said, a city at the foot of a mountain whose brooding and insular dwellers had never really come to terms with the free-wheeling ways of an open city. It was claimed by its hinterland, said others, by peasants and sons of peasants who arrived at its gates from the silent and remote villages in the south and the Bekaa Valley, from other rural parts of this small country, and who brought to the city the attitudes of men uprooted from the land and hurled into a city whose ways were alien to them.

It was a "garden without fences" one obituary read. It was too open; it lay at the mercy of outsiders; in a world of states and a region with cruel politics, the sects of Lebanon had never bothered to build a strong state of their own. The Lebanese prided themselves on their wild and anarchic ways. Then outsiders came: Palestinians and Israelis, Syrians and Iranians, with resources and ideas of their own. And the city and the country around it became a free-fire zone, a battleground for outsiders.

In another eulogy of the city, it was noted that Beirut, modern Beirut, had emerged in the nineteenth century, and had been made grand by Western commerce and culture and had collapsed in the late 1970s and early '80s at a time of great feuding between the West and the Muslim world. To survive Beirut needed the indulgence of the world to its east, the protection and the support of the world across the Mediterranean. And from the time of its rise as a major city in the middle years of the nineteenth century until its collapse, these ingredients were there for the city. At the edge of the Arabian world, Beirut was the entrepot, the Levantine city of middlemen and traders, the gateway to the Syrian interior. Purity was not for this city; this was a city anxious to please and to mimic the ways of the West.

By the early 1980s, in the city that had parodied Paris there was now a parody of Iran's theocratic revolution; parody had replaced parody. Beirut had been a place in which Westerners recognized fragments of their own world. The city was "bastard French," as T.E. Lawrence called it some six decades ago. The city had prospered at a time when the world of Greater Syria had slipped into the orbit of the West. Then there came a time a few years ago when the "hunters of foreigners" (the expression is that of a Lebanese paper) roamed the streets of Beirut looking for Westerners: the grim business of holding hostages had begun after all hope for the city had been extinguished in 1984. The kidnappers picked up those they could find in Beirut after a decade of war and destruction. They did pick up the station chief of the Central Intelligence Agency in mid-March of 1984. But the other victims were librarians, journalists, hospital administrators, missionaries and priests, converts to Islam who had spent many years in Lebanon and who were convinced they had a private affair with the country. It was open season against Westerners. The city once anxious to please had become a forbidden place. In Beirut the veneer of civilization had cracked.

It was easy work for the eulogists, easy to see, in retrospect, the flaws of the city's and the country's origins, the dangers that attended the place, the fury that lurked underneath the tranquility and the pretensions. Lebanon had been in the throes of war since 1975. And Lebanon's war had become a war without end, without a turning point. Several years into the war, no one bothered to count the cease-fires anymore. All of them, all the cease-fires—183 by one count of 1982 or 1983—had broken down. The Lebanese were dying for patches that no longer mattered. Foreign armies had come, but there was no solution to the country's ordeal. At first, in the early 1970s, the Palestinians had made themselves a party to the country's politics. The Palestinian refugee camps which had housed waves of Palestinians who had come to Lebanon in distress following the Arab–Israeli wars of 1948 and 1967 were turned into independent and armed sanctuaries. Then the Syrians had come in full force in 1976; they came to cap the disorder, they said, to prevent the establishment on their Western border of a republic dominated by the Lebanese left and the Palestinians, to rescue the embattled Christians. Like a magnet the presence of the Syrians and the Palestinians pulled Israel across the border. There had been one Israeli invasion in 1978; then there was the terrible summer of 1982 when Israel launched a full-scale war, and took the war to the center of Beirut. The city had been subjected to a long siege from mid-June until late in August. Then came the moment of the Americans in the fall of 1982. The U.S. Marines were dispatched to Lebanon to train a Lebanese army, to prop up a pro-Western regime. But that venture too had failed. Eighteen months later, America gave up on Lebanon. The country was beyond redemption. It had become a land of cruelty and hatred.

The city's great myth—that it was a place where Islam and Christianity met and fashioned a society of compromise—had collapsed. A line ran through the city; the "green line" it was called. In the eastern sector of the city there was a Christian society on its own, ruled by Christian militias. In the western sector of the city, which once housed the Western enclave—the American University of Beirut, the beach-front hotels, the cultural institutions, the embassies—there were competing claimants. On this part of the divide the Palestinians had been in the ascendency before 1982. Their rule had been inherited by the Shia squatters, by neighborhood militias and gangs: here a Druze alleyway, there a quarter dominated by a Sunni militia, here men who answered to the Palestine Liberation Organization, there a group inspired and sustained by Iran's revolutionary regime. In the past the lines in Beirut broke down, ran into the world of other communities. Now men wanted a whole world of their own, amidst their kinsmen.

After a decade of slaughter, the world had tired of Beirut; it had been a city that served others, and it no longer did so. There was a time when Beirut had been a city of middlemen, a city of transit between the West and the Arab world. Now in the Arabian Peninsula, men with wealth had built instant cities in the desert. These cities may have been soulless, but they were safe and orderly and antiseptic. The great oil industry demanded nothing more. In the Peninsula a marriage had taken place between the push-button culture of the West and the austere ways of a desert society. Unlike Beirut, which had bowed to the outsider, assimilated his ways, or at least tried to, the cities in the desert were receiving the West on their own terms, or so they wanted to believe. At any rate, the cities in the desert no longer needed the city of the Levant to interpret and mediate the world for them; they had their own traffic with the outside world. And their people had lost the awe with which they once viewed the great cities of Europe. Arabs, large numbers of them, had found their way to London; they had made that city a familiar place. Beirut had receded into memory, a place which an older generation of Arabs recalled as having once been their second home.

For Beirut, there was another cruel irony. In the 1950s and 1960s, Cairo had been the quintessential radical city, "socialist," austere, engaged in a great revolt against the West. By the time Beirut had collapsed, Cairo had made its peace with the West. And in the city of Islam and Africa and Pan-Arabism, the city which had once harangued those who succumbed to the West, there was a mimicry of things Western, and a vast American presence. The "American Raj" had come to Cairo, the purists said. But Cairo had had its rebellion against Europe and America, its crusade against Israel. And all that had ended in defeat and futility. An army officer from the Nile delta, Anwar el Sadat, had negotiated the terms of Egypt's reconciliation with its enemies; the reconciliation may have been a deed of surrender. Egypt was exhausted and economically ruined. But Sadat had pulled off the deed of surrender with style, and the society over which he presided acquiesced in what he did. Men in Cairo had warred against the world. Now they were anxious to join it.

Even Damascus, the city of soldiers and political intrigue, the city that had kept the world at bay for so long, had come to know a measure of peace and sanity. It was the soldier's peace to be sure, intolerant of dissent, stern, culturally uniform. But a city of unpredictable political moods had been tamed: it had traded its wild political ways for order. And that order rested on a mix of the soldier's vigilance and the merchant's willingness to come to terms with the sultan in return for stability and caution. There were no great cultural pretensions and claims in the Damascus of the late 1970s and early 1980s. Countryside boys from the military, the bearers of a long history of deprivation, the children of an exotic religious sect—the Alawi faith from the mountainous hinterland of Syria—had usurped power and had imposed their will on a city that viewed them with contempt. In time Damascus, the proud city of orthodox Sunni Islam had learned to swallow its pride, to accept the rule of the despised soldiers. And the city with the merciless soldiers in command had succeeded in making itself a power to be reckoned with in the affairs of the region. It was tyranny or anarchy, the Damascus soldiers said, and Damascus had made its choice.

Tyranny and orthodoxy needed a foil, some place of ruin to be held up as an example of places that played with fire. In the stern military republics of the Arab world, in the conservative monarchies determined to shore up an old and familiar world, Beirut was to become the foil, the nemesis waiting to overtake those who succumb to political delirium and illusion.

Before the fall, before the terrible "events" and the political ruin of the last decade, there were tales of Lebanon; tales of a small, mountainous country by the Mediterranean; of Beirut, the charmed city where a dramatic mountain range descended to the sea. There were tales of an enterprising people who lived by their wits and who reconciled the austere Arabian–Islamic truth of their East with the ways and truth of the West.

There were two sets of tales that defined the character and the vocation of Lebanon: tales of the mountain and tales of the sea. The tales of the mountain spoke of the "fastness" of Mount Lebanon—the coastal mountain range that extended from the city of Tripoli in the north to the city of Sidon in the south—of the proud and free villages hanging at the edges of precipices, of the men who squeezed a living out of a harsh soil, of the religious and political freedom of the mountain. In the plains below, in the world of Greater Syria of which Lebanon had long been a fragment, tyranny and uniformity reigned. The rebels, the dissidents, the religious minorities, the men and women with strong wills sought refuge in Lebanon's impenetrable mountain range. And there in a world that successive Muslim states could not subdue, free men of diverse faiths, Christian and Muslim schismatics alike, constructed a world of their own. The lowland vassal versus the mountain freeman: this was the kind of image that inhabitants of the mountain cherished. The children of the mountain, it was said, looked down on events, defied history, ignored fortune, lived close to nature.

The tales of the sea evoked ancestors that the Lebanese identified with: the Phoenician seafarers and their once-prosperous kingdoms on the Mediterranean seaboard. Brilliant men, these Phoenicians were, their history said. On Lebanon's coast, in cities like Tyre and Sidon and Byblos—cities glamored by historical romance but long since diminished—The Phoenicians built thriving realms. They were adventurers and merchants: The Phoenicians had taken the alphabet to remote places; they had taken the first olive tree to Greece. Homer supposedly said of them that they were men skilled in all things; they were a people of practical bent, the Phoenicians.

And their genius for commerce, their wanderlust had been bequeathed to their modern-day inheritors, the Lebanese. The sea had also brought to Lebanon all the people and races of the Mediterranean: "all the dregs, all the flower of rival civilizations are driven to this corner of the Phoenician seaboard," a missionary scholar of Syria and of Islam wrote. On this seaboard, a polyglot world, a hybrid culture, had emerged.

In so many ways the tales of the mountain and the sea were bits of consolation: Lebanon was a hard and poor land. In the folklore of the country, the Lebanese celebrated the beauty and bounty of their land; they spoke of the echo of church bells in its valleys, of the wholesomeness of its villages, of mountainous peaks ascending to clear, blue sky. But they knew the harshness of the land, and saw through the consolation. "How did you find Lebanon," Kahlil Gibran, (1883–1931) wrote to a friend who had returned to Lebanon after a long absence: "Did you find it as lovely as your imagination and yearning had made it out to be, or did you find it a barren land of complacency? Was it the mountain celebrated by poets ranging from David to Solomon to Isaiah to Lamartine, or a multitude of silent and brooding hills and valleys?" Gibran had left the country as a young boy of eleven. His mother had deserted her husband and made her way with her children to south Boston. Far away from the land of his birth—in New York City where he did his work—the sensitive poet had constructed a mythical country, an antidote to what he had known in Lebanon: the cruel, mocking father he had, the poverty, the hierarchies of class. In Boston, his mother and two of his siblings had died of TB. But Gibran's countrymen had preferred to see the story of Kahlil Gibran as evidence of the country's genius: a native son going to a great distant land, taking to that land Lebanon's gift for the tender story and for the poem.

The Lebanese needed the consolation of these tales: deep down, they knew the difficult material of their country. Take that Phoenician past that was never really probed by those who held it up to give the place a usable history. The Phoenician cities had been feuding and jealous entities, they never looked beyond tomorrow, and were cut off from the hinterland around them. The Phoenician world had been a very fragile world. If meditated upon, the Phoenician story would have been one of heartbreak. But the connection between Lebanon and Phoenicia was made to console the desperate Lebanese being pushed out to the New World to make their fortune, to feed the ones who stayed behind. A tale of poverty was thus made into one of grandeur and triumph. This is how Lebanon did things.

Of their country, the Lebanese said that it was an old land: this was what the talk of the mountain and Phoenicia was about. They said of it that it was mentioned in the Bible seventy-five times; they spoke of the foreign conquerors who came and went. In reality Lebanon—within its current borders—was a new country. It was put together in 1920 in the aftermath of World War I and the collapse of the Ottoman Empire. It was a patchwork that brought into the same polity small worlds of differing political traditions and histories. The crucial role in the creation of the new state was played by France which had been granted a mandate over Syria and Lebanon in the scramble for power and territory that followed the First World War. To the mountainous heartland of the country, Mount Lebanon, with its Druze and Maronite "nations" were added the coastal cities of Sidon, Tripoli, and Beirut with their Muslim Sunni populations, and the hinterlands in the south and the Bekaa Valley with their Muslim Shia peasantry. This was to be the quintessential polity of minorities and refugees, some sixteen or seventeen religious sects within the same small republic. In addition to the Maronites and the Druze of the mountain, and the two Muslim sects, the Sunnis and the Shia, there were the Greek

Orthodox and the Greek Catholics and the Syrian Catholics, the Chaldeans and the Protestants, the Orthodox (Gregorian) Armenians and the Catholic Armenians, and a small Jewish community. There were other communities. Men were deeply conscious of their differences here. They had their memories and antagonisms and phobias, and the small republic was to bear the weight of all these obsessions and differences.

The story of Lebanon today is principally that of its capital city. The politics of this small country have become the politics of an extended city-state. But properly the story begins with Mount Lebanon, the heartland of the country.

The world of the mountain had been a world unto itself. Over the course of the four centuries when the Ottoman Empire dominated most of the world of Islam (from the early years of the sixteenth century until the collapse of the Empire in World War I), there developed in the mountain a tradition of political autonomy, an economy of peasant freeholders, a princely state, the *Imarah*, which administered the mountain and which, during periods of power and self-confidence, extended to other parts of Ottoman Syria.

The history of the mountain was, above all, the history of its dominant communities, the Druze and the Christian Maronites. Both religious faiths were faiths of obsession, of purity; both were religions of secluded places and impenetrable mountains.

The origins of the Druze faith are relatively obscure. It began as a schism within a schism in Islam, beginning in Egypt. Al-Hakim, who ruled from 996 to 1021, was one of Egypt's eccentric Ismaili rulers (the Ismailis are a breakaway sect from the Shia sect of Islam). He had come to favor a new revelation and to see himself as the emanation of God in his unity. There were many sides to al-Hakim: he was as religiously inspired and austere as he was, in one historian's words, subject to "bizarre moods and fits of cruelty." He frowned on luxury and

mounted a simple donkey for his excursions. Then one night al-Hakim rode unattended into the desert never to be heard from again. His followers picked up the torch, insisting that al-Hakim would return, but they were soon suppressed in Egypt. That kind of millenarian faith could not survive in the ordered world of a riverbed civilization like Egypt, so the true believers made their way to the hill country of southeastern Lebanon. One of the leaders of this sect was a preacher by the name of Muhammad Ibn Ismail al Darazi. His followers are still known, after him, as Druze. (The name Unitarians has also been attached to the Druze due to their emphasis on the unity of God).

"There are religions of place or race, and religions of doctrine," an observer of the Druze wrote. And this was to be a religion of a particular breed of men and a particular place. The Druze faith had made it to Lebanon after it had been extinguished elsewhere. In its new habitat the Druze faith incorporated a range of esoteric doctrines: belief in the transmigration of souls, in the number of universal principles, in supernatural hierarchies ranked below al-Hakim and his emanation of God. And at some point in the mid-eleventh century, soon after the arrival of the sect in Lebanon, the "door of salvation" and conversion was closed. Henceforth the Druze faith became a hereditary privilege, a "sacred deposit, a priceless treasure to be guarded from profane curiosity."

The teachings and mysteries of the Druze faith were not be revealed to outsiders: "Whoever shall be known to reveal anything of them, let him be put to death without pity. . . . The readings of the mysteries must take place in a secret place, and only in the presence of Unitarians. . . . The books of the mysteries must never be allowed to be taken out of the place of their deposit." The Druze practiced a form of *Taqiyya*, dissimulation. Truth, a sacred obligation among the brethren was to be denied others: "You are not obliged, brethren, to observe truth towards men who are in ignorance, blindness or obscurity. . . . Truth is only obligatory amongst yourselves." In the twentieth century, a Druze chieftain, Kamal Junblatt (assassinated in 1977), said this of his people: "Prudence is another of the distinguishing traits of the Druzes. They don't shout in the wind; ever alert, they gauge their surroundings and choose their words carefully, assessing what must be said and what can be said."

They had always been a martial community, the Druze, governed by a warrior aristocracy, held together by sacred bonds of loyalty and obligations. Masters in the Shuf mountains, the southeastern hills of Mount Lebanon overlooking the city of Beirut, the Druze look back to a time in history (the sixteenth, seventeenth and eighteenth centuries) when they ruled much of this small fragment of Greater Syria around them. Marked out by a special Arabic dialect, by an inheritance and a tradition all their own, the Druze guard the realm left them with zeal and devotion.

For the Maronites, too, place and faith are inextricably linked. And the place, Mount Lebanon, assumes a deeply religious meaning. For them, too, there is a tale of flight from an exposed place to the security and purity of the mountains of Lebanon. In the case of the Maronites, the flight was from the valley of the Orontes River, in Syria, between the cities of Homs and Hama. There, in the last decades of the sixth century, they had been organized as a church by a priest-chief John Maron. Because the Maronites had their own independent Christology, they ran afoul of Byzantine orthodoxy which dominated Syria. Maronite history has been described as one of flight from the Islamic state that conquered Syria between 634 and 641. More likely, the early Maronite struggle had been with the Byzantine orthodoxy. What is clear is that the Maronite base in the Orontes Valley was lost, and that there had been a Maronite migration to northern Lebanon. In Maronite history it was an abbot by the name of Yuhanna Marun who led the flight to the mountains of Lebanon. The persecution in the Orontes Valley, the flight, then the freedom in Lebanon's secluded mountains were to become the basic themes of Maronite history and identity. In time there developed another powerful theme in the Maronite world: the links with Western Christendom, with France and with the Holy See. The links had been established during the Crusades. Muslim detractors of the Maronites and the Maronites themselves, relate how the sect had welcomed the Crusaders, made common cause with them. The chronicles of the Crusades tell of the Maronites descending from the mountains to greet the Crusaders, to guide them on their march to Jerusalem. But reality was not quite so simple: some Maronites, it would appear, sided with the Crusaders while others did not.

In 1180 there occurred a profound change in Maronite history: the Crusaders had prevailed upon the Maronites to accept union with Rome. A Frankish historian by the name of William of Tyre described the event as a "wonderful change of heart." But the Maronites were men of independent temperament, despite the union with Rome, they kept their own fasts and saints and Syriac liturgy. And Rome had to acknowledge the independence of the Maronite Church, grant the Maronite Patriarch the title of "Patriarch of Antioch and All the East." However out of the traffic with Rome and the Crusader kingdoms, a special bond was forged between the Maronites and the French who played a preeminent role in the life and courts of the Crusader kingdoms. As early as 1250, Saint Louis IX, King of France, would say this of the Maronites: "We are persuaded that this nation, which we find established here under the name of St. Marun, is a part of the French nation, for its love for France resembles the love which Frenchmen bear one another." A monarch's hyperbole about an exotic people in a foreign land? For the Maronites, it was much more than that.

In the final years of the thirteenth century, the Crusader

kingdoms were defeated and expelled. But the Maronite bonds with Rome and France survived. In 1515 Pope Leo X said of the Maronites the sort of thing that they treasured: the Pope praised the Maronites as "a rose among thorns." In 1535 there had been a concession made to the French monarch Francis I by the Ottoman Sultan Suleiman the Magnificent, according the French the right to be the protectors of the Christians of the East. The deed, in retrospect, the beginnings of the Ottoman "capitulations" to Europe, had no immediate consequences for the Maronites. But it fed the popular imagination of a small community in Lebanon's mountains; it gave it the conviction that a great Christian power had become its patron and its protector.

Traffic with the Holy See also continued. In 1584 a Maronite college was established in Rome to train and educate a clergy for the Maronite Church. Its first entering class had nine students. More students were to follow. From among the ranks of the college of Rome's students were to come a long line of the Church's patriarchs. A clerical tradition had emerged among the Maronites, with the clergy as defenders of the faith, as educators. Comte C.F. de Volney, a Frenchman who took his inheritance and travelled through Egypt and Syria in the late eighteenth century, found a Maronite church of great power: "Italy itself," he wrote, "has not more bishops than this little corner of Syria. Unlike the monks and priests the bishops constantly engage in cabals . . . and throw the whole country in commotion. In the small country of the Maronites there are reckoned upwards of 200 convents, for men and women." The priests were held in great esteem, Volney wrote: "Their vanity is incessantly flattered; whoever approaches them is anxious to kiss their hands, which they fail not to present."

The ties to France and the traffic with the Holy See would come in handy for the Maronites over the course of the nineteenth century. To begin with, Western power was now a decisive factor in the affairs of the Ottoman empire. Trade with Europe was also expanding, this was a world slipping into the orbit of the European powers. In Mount Lebanon and in the economy of Beirut, silk was becoming the mainstay of the economy. A middle class of Christian entrepreneurs was emerging. Maronites were leaving their mulberry groves to become silk factors and brokers. This was another case of an agrarian, feudal society awakening to new opportunities, giving peasants who tilled the land a chance to break from the hold and power of the landlords. To the thorny class troubles between landlord and peasant were added communal troubles: the Maronite peasants and entrepreneurs were spreading into the Druze districts in the southern portion of the mountain. Maronite society was in the throes of a historic change; the Druze society and its warrior aristocracy were thrown on the defensive. It all came to a bloody communal war in 1860 between the Maronites and the Druze. The Maronites held the numerical advantage. But the Druze social structure—the solidarity, the unity of command—prevailed. Thousands were massacred; by most estimates, some ten thousand Christians may have perished.

Rescue for the Christians came from France. For Louis Napoleon (Napoleon III), this was a chance to pose as "protector of the Christians of the East." There was the shadow of his uncle, Napoleon Bonaparte, who had dreamt of an Eastern empire stretching from Egypt to the Indus. "Everything here passes away; my glory is already declining," Bonaparte had said before he had set out to conquer Egypt at age thirty. "This little corner of Europe is too small to supply it. We must go to the East. All the great men of the world have there acquired their celebrity." The east was the "nursery of kings." For the ambitious general the romance of the Nile Valley led to the romance of India, and to the dream of a vast empire. Napoleon Bonaparte had arrived in Egypt in 1798 with his army, and a team of scientists and savants, to study and "document" the country. But the dream was not to be: his fleet was destroyed by the British, and the venture stalled and withered away. And less than eleven months after he landed in Egypt, Napoleon had deserted his army and slipped back to France. The dream thwarted, its memory and romance had survived, and Louis Napoleon had inherited that particular bit of romance along with the other trappings of Bonaparte's reign. And there was the competition with England for dominance in Ottoman affairs, and with Tsarist Russia for trusteeship over the holy places in Jerusalem and over the Christians of the East. Tsarist Russia's wards here were the Greek orthodox; the Catholics were wards of France. The French expedition in 1860 was intended to underscore the primacy of France in the Levant.

French military intervention set the stage for a new regime for the mountain. Mount Lebanon would become an autonomous province. In name the province would still remain a part of the Ottoman Empire; in reality it had become a protectorate of the European powers. The regime was guaranteed by the combined international support of France, Russia, Britain, Austria, Prussia and Sardinia. This regime bought a measure of peace for Mount Lebanon and was to last until the outbreak of World War I: it was followed by a brutal Ottoman regime of occupation during the years of the war and then by the establishment by the French of the state of Greater Lebanon in 1920. Above all, the international regime sought to bring peace between the Druze and the Maronites.

With peace came a measure of prosperity: a boom in the silk industry brought to the mountain, and to the city of Beirut European merchants and financiers. It was silk production and the commerce in silk which sustained the economy of the mountain and the commerce of Beirut. The mulberry trees which fed the silkworms had been part of the romance of the mountain. The trees paid the taxes, kept alive the love of labor, conferred independence of character. In the spring,

before the silkworms devoured the mulberry leaves, the terraced hills of the mountain must have been a stunning view to behold. The view of the mulberry leaves in bloom is recounted in all the travellers' accounts of the mid- and late 1800s. Half of the cultivated land in the mountain was claimed by the mulberry trees.

Thanks to the commerce in silk and the traffic with Europe, Beirut was transformed from an insignificant port town into a major city of trade. As late as 1820, it was a port town with a population of 6,000; by the end of the century it had become a thriving city with a population of 120,000. Beirut out-stripped its rivals, the coastal towns of Sidon to its south and Tripoli to its north: Sidon and Tripoli remained towns of Islam, towns that looked eastward. Beirut took in the ways of the West and its emissaries—the travellers, the consulates, the religious and educational missions, the merchants. The Beirut of the 1820s had been an old port town with centuries of neglect behind it, a small township with gates that closed at night, with a belt of outer watchtowers, and a scattering of people who lived beyond the city walls. Here is an account of Beirut, through the eyes of an American missionary, William Goodell, from Templeton, Massachusetts, in a January 1824 letter he sent back home:

The place in which providence has cast our lot is pleasantly situated on the western side of a large bay. On the south is a large and beautiful plain, varied by hills covered with olive, palm, orange, lemon, pine and mulberry trees. From the terrace of the house we occupy we can count, without the walls of the city, no less than 200 cottages, scattered here and there in the fields of mulberry trees.

The old city inside the walls was a different story. It was a dirty place: "When I have had occasion to enter the gates at an early hour . . . I have deemed it prudent to tie a handkerchief over my face for the preservation of my health."

More than thirty years later, another missionary, W. M. Thomson, in a celebrated book of commentary and travel, *The Land and the Book*, wrote of Beirut in the midst of a boom: "Thirty years ago there was scarcely a decent house outside of the walls; now two-thirds of the population reside in the gardens, and hundreds of convenient dwellings, and not a few large and noble mansions adorn the charming suburbs. No city in Syria, perhaps none in the Turkish empire, has had so rapid an expansion. And it must continue to grow and prosper . . ." The city's grace had survived the boom. Taking in the deep bay at the base of the hills, and the mountains shaded with pine forests and dotted with villages, Thomson wrote of an enchanting city: "This is Beirut, with the glorious Mediterranean all around, and ships and boats of various nations and picturesque patterns sailing or at rest. You will travel far ere you find a prospect of equal variety, beauty and magnificence."

The city walls were pushed aside. The port facilities were expanded to handle the steamer traffic. By 1863 Beirut was served by seven sea routes. As in the Greco-Roman centuries before the rise of Islam and its conquest of the world of Syria, the coastal world of Syria had once again turned westward; Beirut was the great beneficiary of this shift. Travellers who came by sea felt at home here. Mark Twain making his voyage to Europe and the Levant in the late 1860s (a journey recorded in his book *Innocents Abroad*) saw Beirut as a "beautiful city" with "bright, new houses nestled among a wilderness of green shrubbery spread abroad over an upland that sloped gently down to the sea." Twain was on his way inland to Damascus, a city he described with awe and hostility: "It was the most fanatical Muhammadan purgatory out of Arabia," he wrote. Its people, he said, "so hate the very sight of a foreign Christian." For Europeans and Americans making their way to the Syrian interior, Beirut, the city on the coast, was a place easy to master.

The city was not "fully eastern," according to Western travellers who came to Beirut after seeing other Muslim realms and cities. Following is from one traveller's account of the mid-1870s:

> This sense of entering a place no longer Eastern in its full meaning is new to us. The neat house-fronts, the red tiles, the blooming verandah, said it; the smoke from many a dwelling spoke only of Europe; and the great sea, which laughed and caressed the keels of the many ships, said it too.

The world of Beirut was being re-cast in the image of Europe. There would be winners and losers in a city accommodating itself to new masters. A historian of Beirut, Leila Tarazi Fawaz, cuts through the story and the statistics with remarkable grace and brevity in her book *Merchants and Migrants in Nineteenth Century Beirut*: the commerce of the city with Lyons and Marseilles, the coming of Protestant and Catholic missions, the whole thrust of the economic and cultural traffic across the Mediterranean, tipped the balance of power in favor of the Christian population of Beirut and against the Muslims. Here and there, there were some Muslim families who could traffic with Europeans. But overwhelmingly the advantage belonged to the local Christians dealing with their co-religionists. "The Muslims," historian Fawaz writes, "found it hard to accept the advantages accruing to their Christian neighbors and not to themselves. They had always been on top and saw their superiority as natural. Now the tables were turned, the times were out of joint, and Christian appetites grew with the eating, the more so as the new emigrants from the mountain came devoid of the urban instinct for co-existence and compromise."

It was not only in the realm of culture and commerce that the Christians would prevail: the demographic balance was altered by the boom of the mid-nineteenth century. There had been a rough equality in numbers between the Muslims and Christians in the 1840s. A quarter-century later the Christians were to constitute a two-third majority of the city and they were to retain their demographic edge for the rest of the century. Migration to Beirut—and its sectarian character—had helped alter the demographic balance of the city. Political and religious troubles in the Syrian interior, troubles in cities like Aleppo and Damascus in the 1850s and 60s, and insecurity in Mount Lebanon as a result of the deepening feud between the Maronites and the Druze brought greater numbers of Christian refugees to Beirut. For the Christians of the world of Syria, Beirut was to become the city of refuge.

Moreover, the new Christian migration to Beirut had another break with the past: the old Beiruti Christians had been Greek Orthodox; the new arrivals were Maronites. The Greek Orthodox—heirs of Byzantium, men with a wider sense of belonging to a large Syrian entity—had been men and women of the city: they had shared its life with the Muslim Sunnis. The two communities, the Sunnis and the Greek Orthodox, had known and accepted one another. The Greek Orthodox had the temperament and the ways of the city. The new Maronite arrivals were at heart men of the mountain. The Greek Orthodox had learned how to bend with the wind. They knew, as it were, how to walk the narrow streets and alleyways of a city of rival cultures. The Maronites had been strangers to the city; to the new city they brought the ways and outlook of their sheltered villages.

Beirut was the city that brought men and communities together; its world was formed by their passions, by their sectarian antagonisms. It could not have been otherwise. Men ventured outside the cocoon of their own sect and its certainties and prejudices, but the world of one's kinsmen always beckoned, and the small space on which men of different faiths met cracked during times of trouble. We have a glimpse of Beirut in the early years of this century in a memoir

of a resident, Edward Atiyah, a Protestant, an Oxford-educated scholar and teacher. Atiyah was born in 1903, his memoir *An Arab Tells His Story* (published in 1946) is remarkably candid about the city in which he spent his formative and early years: "A Mohammedan murdering a Christian, or a Christian murdering a Mohammedan—an endless vendetta, one long record of animosity, suspicion, aggression and retaliation, a haunting sense of insecurity. . . . By the time I was eight or nine I had developed, or rather inherited, a definite outlook, common to all the Syrian Christians of the time, a feeling of aversion for the Moslems and the Druzes, whom I had learned to consider as our natural enemies. I felt that there was something alien and uncouth about them, that in some strange way they were not ordinary people like us." Beirut's lines were even more sharply drawn. The writer, being a Protestant, had a sense of separation from the other Christian communities: "In a milder way I was conscious of the differences among the Christians themselves. I knew that there were different sorts of Christians—Christians who were in the right (i.e. Protestants) and Christians who were in the wrong, whose priests wore funeral clothes, large bushy beards, and tall black hats, from which they seemed inseparable."

In Atiyah's rendition, the city's natural beauty is contrasted with what men had done with that gift of nature. And Atiyah's despair is nearly overwhelming. For all its "natural beauty" Beirut, he wrote, seemed "incapable of breeding anything but fear and suspicion and hateful strife." There the city was, "between the blue sky above and the bluer sea below," with the "towering shoulders of the mountain in their cloak of virgin snow" in view; and there in the "shadow of that noble sanctuary of nature lay the sordid human sore of Beirut."

The city that was to be the capital of the state of "Greater Lebanon" was a city of contending cultures. But the Maronites who pushed for the enlarged state—for the current borders of the Lebanese state—wanted it as the capital of their republic. For all the romance of the mountain and of the silk industry, the mountain had not been able to feed itself; the silk industry had collapsed. The production of silk—a small cottage industry—had not been able to withstand the competition of Chinese and Japanese producers who managed to manufacture cheaper and better quality thread. The troubles of the silk industry, which became so pronounced in the years before the First World War, helped break the mountain's economy. Between 1900 and 1914, tens of thousands of the mountain's inhabitants had been forced to emigrate to the New World. And during World War I, there had been great misery in the mountain, widespread hunger and starvation. The searing memories of famine and of ruin had endured. Those memories were there, right alongside the boasting about the beauty of the mountain. To survive the mountain needed the city of trade and the food cereals of the plains of the Bekaa Valley.

At the Versailles Peace Conference, the Maronites lobbied for Greater Lebanon. In the scheme of things, it seemed like a halfway decent compromise. There were those in Syria and Lebanon pushing for an Arab kingdom based in Damascus, and there were the "purists," a minority among the Maronites who wanted a small Christian nation backed by French power. In one Maronite summation, unity with Syria meant political death, while a smaller Lebanon confined to the mountain meant economic death. Hence the case for a Greater Lebanon. In a document submitted to the Paris Peace Conference, the lobbyists for Greater Lebanon argued that without the ports of Beirut and Tripoli and the plains of the Bekaa Valley, Lebanon would be "reduced to rocks," would be as large as a "prison yard." They recited the sad history of the mountain— this time without bravado and mystification: "Lebanon's inhabitants, deprived of access to the sea and robbed of the neighboring coastal Lebanon, were condemned by their

isolation to emigrate in order to survive." History, ancient history, was dredged up by the petitioners; the borders, they claimed, "corresponded to a geographic entity which once was Phoenicia." In lobbying the French, the advocates of Greater Lebanon vowed, in the words of the Maronite Patriarch, that the Lebanese state would be a "refuge for all the Christians of the Orient and an abode of undivided fidelity to France."

The Muslims of the coastal cities, of the towns of the shut-out interior, and the influential Greek Orthodox wanted nothing to do with either a French mandate over their political life or with a Lebanese polity in which the Maronites were ascendant. These communities of Lebanon wanted political independence and unity with Syria. But the mandate was not an affair based on the consent of the governed. France's "honor" and her sacrifices during the war, so the argument went, required compensation in the form of colonial posses-sions. The world of Greater Syria, that of Lebanon included, was to be France's share of the Ottoman inheritance. A short-lived "Arab kingdom" based in Damascus (October 1918 to July 1920) was devastated by French armor, the towns on Lebanon's coast, no less than the city of Damascus itself, had to reconcile themselves to French power. The Maronites' tradi-tional foreign patron was now in possession of the land that the advocates of a larger Lebanon wanted.

On September 1, 1920 General Gouraud, the French High Commissioner, proclaimed the creation of Greater Lebanon. The resistance against the French had been broken, and broken with ease. Six weeks earlier, the French army had shattered the "Arab Kingdom" and subdued its capital city of Damascus. It was futile to persist with the dream of Syrian unity and independence. There is a record of that event of September 1, 1920: General Gouraud, in his army uniform, decked with his medals, seated amidst a large gathering of the country's notables surrounded by French soldiers and re-tainers, seated with the Maronite Patriarch on one side, and the Muslim Mufti (religious scholar and judge) on the other. For the Patriarch, the day must have been a day of triumph: he had pushed for the creation of a Lebanese polity with enlarged borders; for him the coming of direct French control over Syria and Lebanon was no doubt the fulfillment of a dream. For the Muslim Mufti, a man from a noted Beirut family, the occasion could only have been a day of sorrow, the imposition of a rule of a Christian power, yet another reminder of the weakness of Islam in the modern world.

The advocates of Greater Lebanon got the land they wanted. Even then, there were those among them who continued to doubt the wisdom of that choice, who would call for the "amputations" of the territories acquired in 1920. These territories that the French attached to Mount Lebanon were predominantly Muslim territories. This was not quite the Christian national home that the Maronites had dreamt of. There was a built-in contradiction between the dream of a viable Lebanon with "natural borders" and the yearning for a Christian national home.

This kind of contradiction could not be wished away. It was not easy to define the character of the new republic. There were competing conceptions of Lebanon as the Lebanese set out on their own when France—diminished by her defeat at the hands of Germany in 1940, challenged in Syria and Lebanon—finally granted the country its independence in 1943. It was hard work even finding a national myth for the country.

The best attempts to define the character of Lebanon were made, over the course of a quarter century, by an influential intellectual and banker, the Roman Catholic Michel Chiha (d. 1954). Chiha was a rationalist who saw Lebanon as a "Mediterranean country" of trade and services, heir to the great Phoenician cities. For Chiha, the Lebanese were to be "friends of the masters of the world," artisans, and traders. Chiha pulled together two of the country's most powerful themes—the mountain and the sea—to elaborate a new myth for the country. Here are some fragments of what he wrote and said to his countrymen:

> The range of the Lebanese mountains is our backbone, in a literal and figurative sense. . . . Geography and history provide the background for the future of Lebanon. There it is at the hub of continents and in the heart of the Ancient World, abounding in high places, clear skies, fruit trees, sweet water, fresh air and beautiful scenery next to that sea which saw the birth, growth, decline and death of dominations and empires.

And in this passage, Chiha gives his view of Lebanon as a crossroads society.

> We are a place where men acclimatize themselves wherever they come from, where civilizations meet, where beliefs, languages and liturgies bow low to each other; a Mediterranean country first and foremost but like the Mediterranean itself, sensitive to every man's poetry.

The talk of "liturgies bowing to each other" notwithstanding, Michel Chiha was no dreamer. He knew the weaknesses of the country, the competing conceptions of it, the dangers that attended it. Chiha knew that the themes he was working with—the Phoenician seafarers, the rugged mountain—were essentially Christian themes, that these themes were anathema to the Muslim Sunni cities, and virtually incomprehensible to the Shia hinterland. His hope for his country was that the multitude of sects would refrain from playing with fire. His hope and the hope of others like him who labored to give the country a semblance of unity was that the different sects would come to accept this polity of minorities and appreciate its fragility. Compromise, the notables of this republic believed, would see the place through. It was in this spirit that the country's notables agreed to parcel out its posts. At first, in 1934, the Presidency was reserved for the Maronites; three years later, the Sunni Muslims were allotted the Prime Ministership; and in 1947, the Shia got the post of Speaker of Parliament.

It fell to two men, a Maronite mountain politician, Bishara al Khuri, and a Muslim Sunni politician, Riad al Solh, to come up with an informal constitution for the Lebanese republic, to see it through its early years. The understanding between the two men, concluded in 1943, was enshrined as "the National Pact." The Maronite Bishara al Khuri was to become the country's first post-independence president, the Sunni Riad al Solh, the prime minister.

Bishara al Khuri and Riad al Solh were an interesting pair: the lawyer Bishara al Khuri—courtly, shrewd, well-dressed—come through in the photos we have of him, his diaries and speeches, as quintessentially a man of the Levant, subtle and worldly, a man who could navigate troubled waters. He was a friend of the British, and he had spent time in Egypt. Beirut, the city in which he practiced his trade as lawyer and politician, had worked its magic on him, softened the hard edges of his mountain ways. Bishara al Khuri knew that the brittle ways of the hardline Maronites could not go very far in the Arab environment around Lebanon. He had no illusions about the French; his friendship with the British had opened his eyes to a harsh fact that his Maronite kinsmen had tried to avoid: that the moment of France in Syria and Lebanon had slipped by. Bishara al Khuri read the collapse of France in 1940 with unsentimental clarity. The great power which had been the Maronite's patron and protector was being diminished. That large Muslim world to Lebanon's east had to be accommodated.

Bishara al Khuri's Muslim Sunni partner, Riad al Solh, (he was assassinated in 1951, some eight years after the country's independence) was the scion of an old notable family with roots in the city of Sidon. He was in every way a man of the urban, Muslim order, a man with poise and self-confidence, heir to a tradition of ruling, of mediating, of property. He was the country's largest tobacco grower and one of its absentee landlords. Like Bishara al Khuri, he too was a practical man, a skilled politician who could harangue a crowd and then strike a deal behind a closed door. This was not the sort of man to tilt into windmills or stick to things that didn't work. He knew that the unity with Syria for which other Sunni Muslims were agitating was not in the cards.

In the pact, the two men pledged themselves to "Lebanonize the Muslims" and "Arabize the Christians," (the language is so very Lebanese, the product of a place when men trusted the word to smother contradictions, postpone the moment of reckoning). Just as the political order in the mountain had required a Maronite-Druze understanding, the new order of the Lebanese polity was based upon a Maronite-Muslim Sunni understanding. In the vision of the National Pact's two architects, the Christians would loosen their dependence on the West, the Muslim Sunnis would refrain from pushing for Arab unity and would accept Lebanon's statehood and independence.

It was assumed that the other sects of Lebanon—the Druze, the Shia, the Greek Orthodox, the Greek Catholics, the Protestants, the Armenian Orthodox, etc.—had nowhere else to go, no other game to play. The arrangement that mattered was between the country's two preeminent sects: the Maronites with their hold in the mountain, their numbers, their Western connection, their elaborate church, their parochial universities and schools, their sense of possession of that mystique called "Lebanonism," and the Muslim Sunnis, the children of the Arab/Muslim world in Lebanon, the inhabitants of the country's three preeminent coastal cities with their urban bourgeoisie and small shopkeepers. For centuries, the Muslim, orthodox Sunnis of the cities had belonged to the universal civilization of Islam. They were of the majority faith in the Muslim world; they shared the faith of the large Islamic states which governed the world of Greater Syria, as they did the bulk of the Muslim world. (Only Iran, from the sixteenth century onward had become a Shia state). All that was being traded away for a junior partnership in an independent Lebanese state in which the Christian Maronites clearly held the pride of place.

In the hinterlands of the country there was a large Shia population. I will say something about the Shia because their story became important in the years to come. They presented no urgent problem in the Lebanon of the 1940s and 1950s. They were a silent and rural population. They were the country's "hewers of wood and drawers of water." They were ruled by feudal lords who were tyrannical in the Shia villages and frightened in the councils of power that met in the great capital city of Beirut. The Shia had their history of dispossession, and their quietism. They were the stepchildren of Islam. In the first century there had been a struggle for the legacy of the Prophet Muhammad: it was the "pious opposition" rallying around the Prophet's family on the one side and the worldly men on the other. The pious opposition had been defeated, and the Prophet's grandson, Imam Hussein, hero and rallying symbol for the opposition, had been cut down in a battle in Kerbala (today's southern Iraq), which had become a great Shia wound, a reminder of the cruelty of the world. The succeeding centuries had brought no relief to the Shia, (literally meaning the partisans) of the Imams, the chosen religious and political leaders of the Shia. The Shia rose in repeated rebellions, but the rebellions were crushed. In the ninth century, so Shia tradition maintains, the twelfth of these saintly successors to the Prophet went into "occultation"— into hiding—invisible to the eyes of "ordinary men," only to return at the "end of time" and fill the earth with justice. Wherever they were in the Muslim world the Shia lived in the

catacombs. They mourned the defeat of virtue and the triumph of the wicked. The great cities of the Muslim world, the great booty that came to Islam, the tale of Islam's triumph and worldly vindication were not for them. They lived only with the consolation that a time would come when the mighty would be humbled and the lowly who kept up the faith would rise and inherit the earth free from oppressors.

Far beyond Lebanon, in Iran, there was a large Shia state, a state converted to Shiism in the sixteenth century by a dynasty of zealous soldiers and saints, a state of the faithful, with holy shrines and great cities and bazaars, about which the Shia of Lebanon could spin yarns. But Iran was far away and the Shia of Lebanon were a people cut off from great power and large ideas. Arriving at the gates of the city of Beirut in the 1940s and 1950s, they were on their best manners, anxious to work, to school their children, to put behind them the legacy of the beaten and impoverished villages of the south and the Bekaa Valley. The militant and proud Lebanonism of the Maronites was not for them. They admired the Maronites, they envied their educational achievements; but they did not know them. They did not share their ideas, nor did they partake of the Arab nationalism of the Sunni cities. Deep down, they suspected that Arab nationalism was an affair of the cities, that it was the old Sunni domination dressed in secular garb. All in all, it was too early for the Shia to think of great political ideas and undertakings.

My family were Shia Muslims. We were a people of the countryside, of gentry background, a large family outgrowing its limited acreage of land. (I was born in 1945; my family had arrived in Beirut when I was three or four years old). We were among the first Shia to come to the city of Beirut in the late 1940s. There had been an earlier passage to Beirut, but it did not take root: members of my family had come to Beirut in the early 1930s. My father and his sisters and brothers had come for schooling. They had settled at the outskirts of West

Beirut. Some of them recall their first home as a large, sprawling house in the middle of an orchard. But not long after their arrival, the house with the orchard was given up, and the boys in Beirut's schools were sent back to the countryside, to be educated in a large regional town nearby our ancestral village. Beirut was too harsh and too alien for them. It was a Muslim Sunni world, and the generation that preceded mine had not been prepared for the passage. Fifteen years later, my family tried it again, but this time the passage was both more urgent and easier: we had the land to our back. There was a new generation that had to be schooled, that had to learn the ways of the city. The generation of my father, uncles, aunts— ten of them in one family—scrambled to find a footing in the city, to pass onto my generation some skills, some education. We were strangers to Beirut's polish, to her missionary schools, to her Levantine manners. We wanted to pass undetected into the modern world of Beirut, to partake of its ways. My father and his brother and sisters were frantic about being accepted in the city. In time they did what so many Lebanese have had to do: they went away to Saudi Arabia, to West Africa. The money they sent home bought land and property and education for my generation.

The city was not ours; it had to be learned. When we arrived in Beirut, it still had the feel of a large town. There were sand dunes on Beirut's southern approaches. And in the northeastern sector of the city when we first moved into a largely Armenian neighborhood, there were orange orchards, a forest of pine trees, two or three strawberry fields. A few years later, this squatter settlement which the Armenians had built up when they came to Lebanon in the aftermath of the First World War was to become a large urban sprawl, a mixed world of Armenians and Shia, some Palestinians as well. Political tragedies had brought the Armenians to Lebanon: some had come in the last years of the nineteenth century following their persecution at the hands of their Ottoman

rulers, the majority had arrived following the First World War and there was still another migration in 1939–40. A large tale of conflict and dispossession had brought the Palestinians here as well. Our journey to Beirut was different: we were walking away from the limits and the harshness of the land. Unlike our Armenian and Palestinian neighbors, our ancestral village was still there. But its world was no longer sufficient and the time had come for us to break with it. We exalted the land and the village but we could not go back, we had to put the distress of our past and its limits behind us.

Growing up in the city, in the mid-1950s, I knew the world of Beirut the way the cable-cars divided it. There was our home in the Armenian-Shia neighborhood—cramped alleyways, the jumbled sounds of a world of transients, the lines between the Shia and the more developed, more skilled Armenian community. A cable-car ride—and a single fare away—was the center of the city: the bazaar, the brothel, the movie houses, the goldsmith's souk, the smart shopping district. This was the heart of the "old town." Much of the old town had been demolished during the First World War; this had not been a culture that valued old and quaint things. When the old souks had been demolished in the spring of 1915, the first blow was struck with a silver pickax: a band had been there for the occasion, all the town's dignitaries were at hand. This was a terrible time of famine, food rationing, and political repression. The Turkish authorities in control of Beirut at the time staged the renovation of the old town as a spectacle and a diversion from the city's troubles. Still, in the mid-1950s, the center of the old city was a place of great charm and energy.

From the city center the streetcars made their way to what I learned and saw to be three distinct worlds. On the highest hill in Beirut, in the eastern sector of the city, there was the Ashrafieh quarter—a Christian world, with imposing parochial schools and churches. The Ashrafieh of my memory is a place of prosperity and order. Its location on a high hill, its relative seclusion from the noise of the city, its predominantly Christian character gave the place an imposing aura.

Opposite Ashrafieh, on the western side of the city but a world apart, was the Basta quarter, the Muslim Sunni stronghold of the city. This neighborhood spilled into a pine forest which urban sprawl eventually disposed of. When I was a boy of ten or eleven the pine forest was still there; it was there when the makeshift amusement park was set up for the first days that followed Ramadan, the Muslim month of fasting. It was there where we as youngsters went to celebrate the feast, in the new clothes which marked the occasion, with the money given to us as part of the ritual of the feast. The world of Basta was a piece of the urban world of Islam: it could have been a fragment of Damascus or Baghdad. There were backgammon players in the side-streets of Basta, neigh-borhood cafes and small mosques. At dusk, men could be seen strolling in their pajamas to visit a neighbor. There were some grand houses with gardens for the Muslim notables of Beirut, for its old merchant families, though the houses too were to go with time. Just as Ashrafieh's truth was Christian, the truth of Basta was that of Pan-Arabism and of Islam.

Ras Beirut, the Bay of Beirut, on the western coastline of the city, was home of the American University of Beirut, of the elegant beach-front hotels, of the Western embassies and libraries, of Hamra Street, Beirut's most modern shopping thoroughfare. When Beirut outgrew its old walls, the western coastline of the city had emerged as home of the hotels which travellers from Europe, and then from America, favored. It was on this coastline that the founders of the American University of Beirut had established their celebrated institution in 1866. Palm trees were planted along the promenade of this coastline. If the culture of Ashrafieh was French and that of Basta devoutly Arab and Muslim, the culture here was Anglo-Saxon, self-consciously so, but definitely a world conscious of the presence of the American University and of its influence.

The films here were American, so were the "snack bars" that were seen by those who frequented them as extensions of America and its ways.

My generation among the Muslims did not feel particularly comfortable with the ways and the language of France; we did not share the Christians' romance with France. A cultural split divided the city: in Christian East Beirut, the admired, foreign culture remained that of France, the prestigious schools taught in French. In Muslim West Beirut, among Muslim Sunnis and Shia alike and among the Palestinians, the dominant foreign language of instruction was English, and the dominant foreign culture that of America—its films, its books, the hip, easy language. The culture of France in the Levant had been claimed by the Christians, preempted if you will. No parvenu could learn French quite the way it should be learned, pronounce it quite the way it should be pronounced. In contrast, the culture of America was more accessible, easier to enter; newly emancipated (Muslim) classes looking for a world beyond their own small world took to America's ways with some ease.

It was Franco-Arab in East Beirut and among the Christians and Anglo-Arab in West Beirut and among the Muslims and the Palestinians. Even Western culture divided itself here, reinforced the sectarian divisions.

The republic would continue to survive and muddle through: this was the feeling of the 1950s; and this feeling continued well into the 1960s. It was a merchant republic. But what of it? It could not be anything else. Its capital city could be entrusted with making Lebanese out of all those men and women of different communities who converged upon it. There were Arab nationalist pamphleteers who were swept up in the passions of Arab nationalism; in the alleyways and cafes and schools of West Beirut, there were those who responded to the fiery and passionate nationalism of the Egyptian President Gamal Abdul Nasser. But they were harmless. This was not a very serious place and there was no use pretending that it was. There were Palestinian refugee camps on the outskirts of Lebanese cities. Some one hundred thousand Palestinians had come to Lebanon in 1948, but they were quiet and subdued, wards of United Nations relief work. In the camps there were memories of Palestine and vows that the Palestinians would return to what they had lost in 1948. And that, too, did not seem so particularly urgent, so particularly seditious. There was a prosperous Palestinian middle class. But they were busy making their way into the professions and the universities, busy with the world of Beirut's finance and its affairs.

Beirut, assuming greater importance in the life of the country, drawing an ever-increasing percentage of the country's population, exuded self-confidence, and savored the good press it received. Military dictatorships were coming to power in the Arab world and the region needed a city where those who lost out in the game of politics could retire, or plot their return to power or write their memoirs. There was oil wealth in the Arabian Peninsula and the Gulf states: this was long before the time the Saudis and Kuwaitis would make their way to London. The wealthy Arabs—puritanical at home—needed a place to play. Beirut became the playground, the easy city, the city with the red-light district and the brothel; the quaint towns in the hills overlooking the city were ideal summer resorts for those fleeing the heat of the Arabian states. The Arab world had an affair with the West, and Beirut would be the city in which the affair could be indulged. The rest—the austere city of Damascus, radical Cairo under Gamal Abdul Nasser, the cities of the Arabian Peninsula—could keep their distance, feign great cultural and political purity. For their part Westerners needed a footing in the Arab world. And Beirut was to be the place.

The spirit of the Levant, that polyglot culture of trade and middlemen of the coastal world of the eastern Mediterra-

nean—the spirit once associated with Alexandria in the 1920s—was making a home here. It was "neither Greek, Syrian nor Egyptian, but a hybrid: a joint," Lawrence Durrell had once written of Alexandria, the site of his fiction. The Levant designated a place. But more, the Levant was a moral and cultural sensibility born of the meeting of rival cultures, of the confusion of men and women forced to walk a tightrope between two worlds. The Oxford (Lebanese-born) historian Albert Hourani has written with great depth and beauty of this splitting of the self that being a Levantine required:

> To be a Levantine is to live in two worlds or more at once, without belonging to either; to be able to go through the external forms which indicate the possession of a certain nationality, religion or culture, without actually possessing it. It is no longer to have a standard of values of one's own, not to be able to create but only able to imitate; and so not even to imitate correctly since that also needs a certain originality. It is to belong to no community and to possess nothing of one's own. It reveals itself in lostness, pretentiousness, cynicism and despair.

A Levantine city, Beirut lived by its wits, with a Swiss-like banking system where Arabs on the run could feather a nest for a rainy day, a capital of trade and services. A keen observer could discern the weakness underneath the polish and the apparent success of the city: Jan Morris, the gifted wanderer and travel writer, knew the city well. Writing in 1956, she could see beyond the "headiness of character" and the irresponsible "gaiety" and the "silken ladies, francophile to their last delicate gasp." "Beirut," she said, "feels a transitory place . . . such a way of life, you feel, cannot be permanent: it is all too fickle, too fast, too make-believe and never-never. . . . Beirut feels a rootless city, virile but infertile. A breath of wind, it seems, a shift of fortune, and all this bright-painted fabric would be whisked away into oblivion, like the countless predecessor cities of this Phoenician shore." This city could not withstand great movements of redemption, or great crusades. To survive, the city had to travel light, broker different truths. From Jan Morris again: "No aesthete could flourish in such a setting, no fervid demagogue could keep it up for long, and all the strident passions of our times, transmuted from violence or grandiloquence, are tamed here into sultry back-chat, boudoir rivalry and skulduggery. . . . This is not an earnest city."

Political trouble—child's play when compared to the violence of the seventies—came to Beirut in 1958. It was caught in the crossfire in a fight between radical Arab nationalism, led by the Egyptian Gamal Abdul Nasser and that great cold warrior Secretary of State John Foster Dulles. A Lebanese president, Camille Chamoun, had done what the founding fathers of this small republic had warned against: he played with fire, he pushed at the seams of the sectarian contract between Muslim and Christian. Tempted by the diplomacy of pacts and alignments that Dulles was prompting in the region, Chamoun threw caution to the wind, sought an alliance with the U.S., with the conservative Arab monarchies of Iraq and Jordan against the radical tide of Arab nationalism. A master of intrigue who wanted to renew his presidential six-year term—excluded by the political constitution and practice of the country—Chamoun rigged a parliamentary election, got rid of his opponents, presented his personal ambitions and feuds as a battle between the West and radical nationalism, between Lebanon's Muslims and Christians. Barricades and weapons appeared in the streets of Beirut. There was a sectarian flavor to the confrontation in 1958. Christian Maronites rallied to Chamoun; the Druze of the Shuf mountain and Muslim West Beirut, Sidon and Tripoli were arrayed against him. Weapons were smuggled from Syria to the Muslim opponents of Camille Chamoun.

In mid-summer 1958, on July 14 to be exact, a coup d'etat took place in Iraq. The pro-Western monarchy was brought down. A young king, his family, his hated prime minister, who was a man of the old school with long ties to British intelligence, were all gunned down by the military. The Hashemite monarchy in Iraq had been a dynasty imposed and sustained, since the 1920s, by British power. Nearly four decades after the British had brought to Iraq a dynasty of outsiders dependent on British protection and patronage, a nationalist generation with roots in the Iraqi middle class had risen to claim power. Two brigades of the Iraqi army passing through the capital on their way to the Syrian frontier had seized their chance on July 14, 1958 and attacked the Royal Palace. The soldiers had put an end to this pro-Western monarchy. The next day the U.S. Marines landed in Lebanon. The Arab friends of the West appeared in great trouble and had to be rescued. A line had to be drawn. There were worries that the King of Jordan, who was a cousin of the King of Iraq, was in imminent danger. There was an American doctrine, the Eisenhower Doctrine, which pledged that "overt armed aggression from any nation controlled by international communism" would be met by "the armed forces of the United States." And it was under the provisions of the Eisenhower Doctrine that U.S. forces were sent to Lebanon.

It was an innocent time. This is from *The New York Times* of July 16, entitled "Little Lebanon is Cosmopolitan," introducing readers to the exotic place to which American forces had gone in defense of freedom:

The republic of Lebanon is the most Westernized country in the Middle East. . . . Lebanon, only a little more than half the size of New Jersey, occupies a strip 120 miles along the eastern end of the Mediterranean Sea between Israel and Syria, and extends inland 30 to 35 miles. . . . The country is comparatively prosperous and enjoys the highest standard of living in the Arab world.

And here is an excerpt from a Beirut dispatch from *The New York Times* of July 17, on the life of the Marines in Lebanon: "Three marines, one carrying a rifle, marched into the bar of the St. George Hotel tonight before the startled eyes of high society customers. Each ordered a beer. They gulped it, then moved along on patrol. One, a sergeant, explained he knew the place because he had been there on leave."

For the U.S. Marines, the story that summer was the unbearable heat of Beirut in the day time and the mosquitoes at night. There were dispatches from Beirut about the heat and the mosquitoes. And soon before the summer came to an end, Chamoun was provided a graceful exit and the country returned to normal. The commander of the Lebanese army, a decent man from a "princely" family, a Maronite, became president, set out to reform the system, restore the balance between Muslim and Christian, guide the country as he had the apolitical army.

There were inequalities in the country. And this was known. In the 1960s men began to speak of these inequalities as though they were seeing them for the first time. And in a way they were. The inequalities had been there; they were as old as the hills of this stubborn land. Mount Lebanon was far more developed than the south, the cities on the coast much more so than the Bekaa Valley in the east with its remote villages with unpaved roads. The education at the American University of Beirut and at Saint Joseph University (founded in 1875) in East Beirut was superior to anything public institutions offered. The sects were unequal and managed somehow to inhabit different, small worlds. The feudal lords and oligarchs of the republic still strutted around, trailed by armed men, by retainers. What was novel was that the inequities were suddenly being seen in a new light.

The discourse changed in the 1960s. Men were awakening to newly perceived inequities. The shantytowns around Beirut were beginning to be noticed. (And soon, in a few years, the shantytown inhabited by Palestinians, by impoverished Shia would have a new and loaded name, the "belt of misery" around the city). The polity's founding fathers had said that Lebanon would not need a strong state, would not need government tinkering in the economy, that the Lebanese genius worked best when it was left without supervision. The banker and intellectual Michel Chiha had expressed this kind of sensibility. Lebanon, he had said, would continue to be an oasis of liberty unless the "ideologists and reformers become strong enough to put an end to it."

At some point in the mid-1960s, more than two decades after the country's independence, this was still the discourse of those who mattered in Lebanon. But doubts were accumulating. There were storms over the horizon. A bank of great power and visibility collapsed in 1966. More of the country's newly educated people—educated with money made in faraway places—were beginning to make new claims. Still, the system could function. And those who praised the country could favorably compare it to the grim military dictatorships in Egypt, Syria and Iraq, with their failed socialism. They could say of it these things they were taught to say: that it was a place where you could ski in the mountains in the mornings and swim in the afternoon, that its press was free and uncensored, that it had a parliament, that presidents were really elected by the parliament for a six-year term after which they actually relinquished power. It wasn't perfect, this small republic by the Mediterranean, but it was better than the alternatives.

Beirut continued to serve, and the Arab world continued to express itself here. Arabic letters thrived in this city. The Arabic book was written in the politically repressive world of Cairo, published in Beirut, and read in the conservative states of the Arabian Peninsula. The press may have been for the hire—the city's large number of newspapers reflected the worldviews of their patrons, the rival embassies and foreign governments that paid and sustained them. But the press still played with ideas, pointed fingers, debated the issues of the region, and now and then appalled the conservative custodians of proper and improper things. The world of Beirut may not have been as free or as brilliant as the nostalgists of later years were to recall it. But it was easy to breathe and to question here; this was a city spared the political orthodoxy and the repression of the radical regimes nearby or the stifling cultural and religious orthodoxy of the states of the Arabian Peninsula.

Then the Six Day War of 1967 broke out. The Egyptian leader and Pan-Arab hero Gamal Abdul Nasser had stumbled into a war with Israel for which he was not prepared. In mid-May of 1967, three weeks before the full-scale eruption of the war, Nasser had mobilized his troops and moved them to the Sinai Peninsula: he had been warned by the Soviets that an Israeli attack against Syria was in the making. Then choosing to push matters further, he had closed the Gulf of Aqaba to Israeli shipping. Israel struck on June 5. And there was that great spectacle of Arab weakness, that defeat, and its verdict on the condition of Arab society. Lebanon had sat out the war. But for the Lebanese, as it was for other Arabs, this was a great divide. The defeat of Egyptian, Jordanian, and Syrian armor, the loss of the West Bank of the Jordan River, the loss of the Sinai Peninsula and the Golan Heights, shattered the myths of a generation of Arabs. A new world beckoned, Arabs had been told before the June defeat of 1967. A new generation had broken with the weaknesses of the past, with the compromises of the *ancien régime*, it was claimed. All this had been put to the test, and then torn to shreds, when the Egyptians and the Syrians had blundered into a war for which they were not prepared.

A more serious and a far grimmer world was to emerge from the June defeat of 1967. The dominant political order in the Arab world was on the defensive. It was hard for the reigning order to check the despair and the cynicism of the young, to check those seeing in the defeat an open invitation to re-constitute the political and cultural life of the Arab world. A multitude of voices clamored to be heard in the aftermath of the defeat. "We haven't been religious enough, Islamic enough to defeat the Jewish State," said the Islamic groups; "We haven't been modern and scientific enough," others asserted; "We haven't applied the theories of revolutionary warfare and the teachings of the 'great masters of guerrilla warfare,' " said the young romantics.

The ideological void created by the defeat of the political order of Arab states was soon filled by the Palestinians. The Palestinian pamphleteers went to work, and the gun-men as well. They vowed that they would reconstitute Arab society, make it more daring, more revolutionary, rid it of its age-old responses and defects. The first Palestinian base was in the Hashemite Kingdom of Jordan, a country with a Palestinian majority. For nearly three years the Palestinians had their moment there, humiliated the monarchy, created a mini-state. But in September 1970, the bedouin forces of King Hussein, loyal to their monarch whom they revere as a descendant of the Prophet, served a warrant on the illusions. It was an all-out war and the Palestinian guerrillas were overwhelmed and banished from Jordan. It was a merciless fight for the country. And King Hussein, who had lost the West Bank to Israel three years earlier, was determined to keep what was left of his modest realm on the east bank of the Jordan River.

Lebanon became the new base for the Palestinian guerrillas. It had a weak state, a relatively large population of Palestinian refugees, an open and permissive political environment. And there, until they were expelled by Menachem Begin and Ariel Sharon in the summer of 1982, the Palestinian fighters acquired a political world with all the trappings: "commanders" who gave press conferences, welfare relief for the Palestinian poor, a mini-capital of sorts in West Beirut. At first, the armed Palestinian presence was modest and hesitant, paying lip service to Lebanese sovereignty, playing cat-and-mouse with the Lebanese army. But a few years down the road, restraint was thrown to the wind. The Palestine Liberation Organization of Yasser Arafat and his lieutenants—a generation of men who watched the flight of their fathers from Palestine in 1948—became a power to be reckoned with in Lebanon. Lebanon, the Palestinians said, was an Arab country, part of the Arab world; they could not accept restrictions on their right to bear arms, to launch incursions into Israel.

The frightened men and women of the refugee camps were given guns and the conviction that the liberation of Palestine had to be waged from Lebanon. There had been a great Palestinian shame, a deep wound left by the Palestinians' flight from their land in 1948. The shame was to be exorcised in Lebanon. As "revolutions" and sanctuaries go, the Palestinian presence in Lebanon was among the most exhibitionist of revolutions: military funerals, posters, colorful uniforms, checkpoints and guns everywhere, all the emblems of defiance. "I never saw a less discreet, less cautious revolution," the Druze leader Kamal Junblatt, and the Palestinians' main ally in Lebanon, observed of the Palestinian guerrillas. That lack of discretion had worked to their ruin in Jordan. It would catch up with them in Lebanon.

Two Palestinian causes were rolled together in the rise of Palestinian power in Lebanon. The aim of the first cause was the standard aim of a national movement: the recovery of a national territory, the restoration of a lost identity. The second cause was fed by entirely different sentiments: the men and women of the camps had risen because they had been resentful spectators to the glitter of Beirut, to the success, to the pretensions; they had envied the propertied and polished classes. The lines here between those who mattered and those who didn't were very clear and the burden of poverty nearly suffocating. Revolt, dressed in the garb of a great national cause, gave marginal men and women in the camps a chance to avenge yesterday's slights and deprivations.

The polish and the glitter and the achievements of the city:

this was a world removed from the crowded camps which supplied Beirut with day-workers, with maids, with men and women who did the lowly work of the city. In the resources and the daring of a new Palestinian movement, the underclass in the camps found the means to vent the grievances of a dispossessed population.

The divisions of Lebanon gave the Palestinians room. At first the Muslims in the country—the Sunnis and the Shia—gave the Palestinian presence their blessing and support. The cause of Palestine was a great Pan-Arab cause, and the Muslims of Lebanon could not walk away from it with ease or indifference. For the Muslim youth of Lebanon, this was a cause with lure and appeal. And the cause of Palestine became linked, in the politics of the late 1960s and early 1970s, with the issue of social and political reform within Lebanon. The Druze, too, fighting their old fight with the Maronites, sided with the Palestinians. Kamal Junblatt, the Druze feudal chief—part pillar of the old order of notables, part overlord of the left in the country—threw his weight behind the Palestinians. The enigmatic Druze politician had a difficult time accepting his place in the Lebanese polity's scheme of things. He was an ambitious man with wide horizons, a well-read man, a philosopher, part mystic and part practitioner of power, yet he belonged to a minority sect, could not aspire to the country's highest posts. The Lebanese state hemmed in his ambitions, and he, in turn, saw the state as a Maronite preserve and privilege. In the Palestinian armed and political presence in Lebanon, Junblatt saw an opportunity to put an end to the Maronite ascendancy.

Among the Maronites there was a growing sense of betrayal: the country they knew was being transformed right before their eyes, its sovereignty emasculated and diminished. This was not quite what the early architects of the grand compromise between the "Lebanonism" of the Maronites and the Pan-Arabism of the Muslims had in mind. With such a fragile state to work with, the Maronites opted for self-help. The proliferation of militias and private armies in the early 1970s was to be the answer to the escalating disorder. At a time of great panic and confusion in the Maronite world, the more militant of the Maronites stepped forth. A familiar world was being threatened. The kind of self-confidence that had placed the Maronites at the center of the Lebanese state had cracked. Most retreated into themselves. Those repressed fears about a small Christian people caught in the midst of an alien Muslim world: the fears had been there and the chaos in Lebanon brought them to the fore. Those memories of the 1860 massacres at the hands of the Druze had been hammered into the Maronite psyche, transmitted from one generation to the other.

Luck had kept Lebanon out of the Arab-Israeli conflict. Hitherto, no one in the Arab world had asked this fragile republic to launch crusades it could not win. But Lebanon had run out of such luck. And soon a deadly pattern was established: Palestinian raids into Israel brought Israeli reprisals into Lebanon. Thousands were pushed from the border villages of the south into the slums of Beirut, into that "belt of misery" around the city. The Lebanese state was being shown to be a scarecrow. No Palestinian tears were shed for the Lebanese state, for the grace of years past. Lebanon had been home for some of them, but there was a political generation convinced of its own vocation. Emancipated by the disorder of the country, the Palestinians pushed on to build a political turf of their own. When the age of nationalism had come to the region, the Palestinians had been left out. In the anarchy of Lebanon, the passion of Palestinian political men to rule, to administer men and things could be satisfied.

A great fortune had come to the Arab world in 1973—the windfall profits of oil wealth due to the quadrupling of the price of oil. The wealth played havoc with the ambitions of men in the Arab world, gave them a sense of a bright new world in the making, ruptured the old limits and restraints by which Arabs lived. The Palestinians, well represented in the wealthy oil states, were well positioned to stake a claim to the new wealth. There was a large Palestinian diaspora, quite skilled and educated, in the states of the Gulf: the Palestinian sanctuary in Lebanon carved out by the Palestine Liberation Organization would be sustained and financed by the Palestinians working in the oil states. And the Arab oil states, too, were generous in their financial contributions to the Palestinian organizations. The new wealth and resources had given the Palestinians a new sense of themselves. But it also highlighted and underlined their peculiar political existence as stateless men and women. If the ruins of Lebanon were to be the new Palestinian turf, so be it. A Palestinian lieutenant of Yasser Arafat, Salah Khalaf, with the code name of Abu Iyad, put it this way in a memoir of his political life, and a set of reflections on the "Lebanese tragedy": the Palestinians, he said, "had no other place to go but Lebanon. If we had to yield, the gains made in decades of struggle would be lost. Of course the Palestinian revolution would ultimately survive, but a decisive defeat in Lebanon would compromise it for years to come." The grandiose claims of the Palestinian revolution versus the mundane case of ordinary Lebanese that they be spared the hell of the Israeli-Palestinian struggle. It was an uneven fight; and it was a fight in which the larger Arab states—zealous in asserting their own sovereignty—were remarkably indulgent of the Palestinians.

Nor was the armed Palestinian presence all that Lebanon had to contend with. There were things Lebanese that had changed, that had to be addressed. There had been a census in 1932, a census conducted under French auspices which established the percentages among the country's population of the different religious sects and parcelled out the political power among the principal sects. No census had been taken since then. But it was known in the way such things are known that the demographic make-up of the country had changed. When the census had been taken the Maronites were the largest sect; they accounted for 29 percent of the country's population. They were trailed by the Sunni Muslims who were 22 percent; and then came the Shia with 19 percent. The other Christian sects and the Druze combined, made up the remaining thirty percent of the country. Anyone with eyes could tell that the assumptions of the old census no longer held. All one had to do to know that the old census had become fiction was to wander into the Shia slums in northeast Beirut, or on the southern approaches to the city. A new urban underclass was there in large numbers, with birth rates far exceeding that of the quiet and prosperous Christian suburbs and towns. In 1975, a daring newspaper, the country's leading paper, *An Nahar*, published its own estimates of the country. The Shia had become the country's largest sect, the Maronites had slipped to third place. The Sunnis were the country's second largest sect after the Shia. Furthermore, the Israeli-Palestinian war in southern Lebanon had forced the Shia of the south into the city. And the city imparted to them its impatience, rid them of the timidity of the countryside.

Chance, too, had sent the way of the Shia a gifted leader, the kind of man who comes a people's way just when he is needed. An Iranian-born mullah by the name of Musa al Sadr arrived in Lebanon in 1959 when he was thirty-one years of age. Tall with striking looks and great ambitions for himself and his flock, Musa al Sadr had set out to reinterpret Shia history, to strip it of its quiescence, to stand the Shia rituals of grief and mourning on their head, to read into the old Shia tales of dispossession a new politics of commitment and daring. In the 1970s, in a situation of breakdown, Musa al Sadr was accorded the extraordinary title of Imam—religious and political leader. As in the more celebrated relationship between the Iranian crowd and Ayatollah Khomeini of the late 1970s, here too, though a few years earlier, a man of religion became the

repository of popular hopes and aspirations. The millennarian theme of the Shia, with its anticipation of an extraordinary individual, was there for Musa al Sadr to draw upon. His gospel of reform, with its subtle mix of humanitarianism and intermittent threats of civil disobedience against the state, was yet another break with the old order and its assumptions.

The country's formal politics—its elaborate political rituals, the shell of the Lebanese state with its president and parliament and cabinet—mattered less and less, answered less of the country's needs. The Palestinian dominion was established in West Beirut and in the south of Lebanon: to be sure it had a Lebanese cover, the "Lebanese National Movement" with Sunni militias in West Beirut, Druze allies in the Shuf Mountains. On the other side, in East Beirut and in Mount Lebanon, the Maronite militias held sway: the Phalange, a party established in the 1930s, the Tigers, a militia headed by a former President, whose middle name, Nimr, meant tiger. The Shia, the country's largest sect, were still on the sidelines: the adventurism of the Palestinians was not to their liking; besides it was on their ancestral land in the south that the Palestinian bravado and caprice played themselves out. Likewise, the Maronite project of defending the Lebanese republic of days past left them indifferent. It was too early for them to stake out their own claim, to take up arms in its pursuit.

A ferocious storm was in the making. In *Beirut: '75*, a novel by Ghada al Samman, (completed in November of 1974), three veiled women—rather like the three witches in Macbeth—cross to Lebanon from Syria and prophesy for the land they glimpse a time of great troubles. "I see great sadness, I see blood, a great deal of blood," one of them said. In the same novel a man escapes from an insane asylum and has this to say about the city: "When I escaped from the asylum the first thing I did was to steal the placard that read 'the asylum of the insane.' I carried the placard to the entrance of Beirut and I removed the sign that carried Beirut's name and in its place I put the other placard."

To the land of trade and services and hotelkeepers, came a new politics of zeal and vengeance. Beirut itself was choking: in 1975–76, when the war waiting to happen finally broke out between the Palestinians (and their Lebanese allies) and the Maronite militias, Greater Beirut accounted for something like 45 percent of the country's population. It was too small and cramped a place to withstand all the political projects, all the fears and passions that swirled around it.

To the extent that Lebanon's war could be dated, the fighting broke out in April of 1975 between the Palestinian organizations and their Lebanese allies on one side and the Maronite militias on the other. The fighting began on a Sunday, April 13: a bus carrying Palestinian passengers was ambushed as it made its way through a Christian suburb of Beirut, and the passengers were killed. Earlier in the day unknown assailants had fired at a church gathering killing the bodyguard of the head of the Maronite-based Phalange party and two others. The ambushing of the bus was a deed of retaliation, and it was the spark for the drawn-out war to come.

Ten days after the ambushing of the bus a woman of Beirut—of a professional middle-class family, Palestinian father, Lebanese mother—records in her diary, *Survival in Beirut*, a small event foreshadowing things to come. She goes to a fashionable jeweler to buy a Koran for her husband to wear around his neck. "So you want to buy a Koran too," the jeweler says. "I don't even know if I have any left. I've sold one hundred and forty in the past week and exactly two-hundred and thirty-three crosses. My whole stock. I've never seen anything like it. Is there a Christian feast? A Moslem feast? I don't understand it at all." Men and women were flaunting their faith and religious identity; they had covered over differences here, now they were asserting them.

Once the fighting began, Lebanon's dirty war acquired its own rules. It degenerated into a war in which the combatants tortured before they killed, maimed the dead, and rarely took prisoners. Massacre followed massacre. Now the victims were Palestinian and Shia dwellers of a slum area called Karantina caught behind Maronite lines and the assailants were young Maronite boys who toasted their victory with champagne and brought the bulldozers to clean up and level the place, to remove any traces of a people to whom these slums had been home. Now the victims were Maronite inhabitants of a quiet town, the town of Damur, on the coastal road to Sidon—a town famed for its bananas and oranges and pottery, a place of memory of my own childhood, a town between Beirut and our ancestral village further south—and the assailants were Palestinians. Damur was ransacked in January 1976; even the oranges in the citrus groves were picked clean. Five hundred men and women may have been killed. The sign at the town's entrance—the sign with the town's name—was altered. Splashed on top of the old name of Damur was a new name, Mudamara, meaning "the destroyed." Right above the new name was scribbled the word Fatah, the name of the Palestine Liberation Organization's largest faction: the victors' calling card. Damur would come to haunt those who prevailed: a particularly zealous and murderous group, the Damur Brigade, was to become the Maronite militias' most vengeful unit. Men were going at it with abandon.

"Cantons" and turfs were being carved out. Woe to those caught in the way. In the summer of 1976, a grim drama unfolded in the northeastern hills overlooking the city. On the hills stood a Palestinian refugee camp with the name Tel Zaatar, the hill of thyme, evocative of an older, more graceful time. Tel Zaatar fell behind Maronite lines. It stood in the way between East Beirut and the Christian-controlled countryside. By the new logic of things, the location of Tel Zaatar was untenable. Prior to the summer of 1976, Tel Zaatar had just been a squatter settlement, a refugee camp. It had sprung up in 1950 when the Palestinian refugees came to Lebanon. At the time, it had a population of 5,000; by 1976, its population had swelled to 15,000. In the summer Tel Zaatar was to become a great tragedy, and a great epic. The "tigers" of former President Camille Chamoun laid siege to it. The siege lasted 52 days; the camp was stormed 72 times before it succumbed. By the time it fell, more than 1,500 had been killed, 4,000 were wounded; barbarous deeds were committed on the day of the camp's surrender, deeds that the Maronite militias acknowledged. These deeds were a revenge, it was said, for the atrocities committed by the Palestinians in the town of Damur: Damur, in its turn, had been a revenge for that ghastly deed committed by Maronite militiamen in Karantina. And so forth.

Ambiguity and compromise had seen the place through early crises. Now compromise had become betrayal and men were looking at the country in a new light, saying things they had not permitted themselves to say. Some Muslims began speaking of an "Islamic state" in Lebanon. And among the Maronites, there was open talk of partitioning the country, walking away from the republic of compromise. In a 1976 pamphlet published by the University of Kaslik for a monastic order headed by a militant monk, Boulos Na'aman, the political life of the country in the preceding half century had been a "tragedy," the co-existence of its Muslims and Christians a "hypocritical farce": "We are drawn to the conclusion that Lebanon in its present form is not viable and that the generation which has been trying to build up a modern state from 1943 up until now has worked in a void. . . . Politically the Christians have lost all initiative since casting their lot with Arabism, and the problems of the Arab world have been settled at their expense. This has caused them to lose the leadership of their own country and to become refugees in it. Their holy places were desecrated,

their forces depleted and their people massacred . . ."

The Lebanese and the Palestinians were digging in for a long war. In the years of tranquility Beirut prided itself on its chic ways. Fashions, the Lebanese used to say, hit the streets of Beirut as soon as they made their appearance in Paris and London. With the war, a particular kind of chic was to come into the place, the manners and attire of a place at war: the elegant battle fatigue, the jungle camouflage uniforms, even Zoro outfits, the holsters over tight blue jeans, the Kalashnikov—the Soviet assault rifle—the jeeps for the commanders. The ruin had come. There had to be consolations and make-believe. Young boys with no future were given guns; "lion-cubs" the boys were called.

Other conquerors who came to this city had left it their monuments and architecture, their ideas, their half-assimilated legacies and skills, their educational missions. The legacy and the gift of the new combatants was to be the spray-paint can, the graffiti on the battered walls: "Fatah was here," "The Communists were here," "The Guardians of the Cedar were here," etc.

In nearby Damascus, the Syrian President Hafez Assad watched Lebanon's chaos. A serious military man who had come to power in a coup d'etat in 1970, Assad was a consummate player of politics. At first he had paid lip service to the "progressive" Palestinian camp in Lebanon; the Syrians fed the flames, provided weapons and support to those undermining the Lebanese state. But by 1976, Assad had switched alliances. The Maronites were on the ropes, and the Syrian president had begun to worry about the emergence of his western border of a radical republic dominated by the Lebanese left and its Palestinian allies. Assad wanted a stalemate in Lebanon, a situation that would give Syria a greater power over Lebanon's affairs. So on June 1, 1976, Assad dispatched his army to Lebanon to the aid of the embattled Maronites. Pushed against the wall, the Syrian president said of the Maronites, they would seek an alliance with Israel, create a "Christian Zion," break with the Arabs. So he, a defender of Arab integrity in the Fertile Crescent, was providing the Maronites with an Arab raft, encouraging them to trust their Arab habitat. The Palestinians, and the "adventurous left," he said, had pushed things to the brink. The Lebanese—with Palestinian help—had squandered their independence. An irresponsible city had to be rescued by the military state to its east.

The politically boisterous and chic city had fallen. A critic of the Syrian regime, the Druze chieftain Kamal Junblatt, said of those who came from Damascus that they came not only to impose their kind of order but to help themselves to the booty of a ruined city. The Syrians, he said "tore through Beirut like a cyclone, looting everything. The flea market was flooded with goods looted from the houses, villas, banks, shops and seraglios of Beirut. After all, Persian carpets are a good long-term investment. . . . The pillage was not quite so accidental as one might think. Lebanon had, after all, been an object of envy throughout the Arab world."

"We don't want the great Syrian prison," said Kamal Junblatt to the military ruler of Damascus. He was speaking for many Lebanese who had been smug about their city and its ways, who viewed Damascus, the city of the hinterland, as a hick-town ruled by military men. But anarchy had stripped Beirut of its pride. The harvest of freedom had been ruin.

A few months after the confrontation between the Syrians and the Druze chieftain, Junblatt and his driver and a companion were struck down. The norm of politics here was that leaders were always spared, or in the imagery of the Levant, that you always shot the horse but not the rider. New political ways were settling in. On the other side of the familiar world, the Lebanese and those Palestinians in their midst were venturing into a political world of cruelty and carnage. In the civil war of 1958 people actually knew and remembered the names of those who fell in battle. And that too was part of a distant past.

For a long time the Lebanese had been saying things they didn't believe in. The violence provided a release from the polite discourse. No one now felt compelled to say that the (Muslim) Crescent and the Cross embraced in Lebanon. And the fury of battle had a certain kind of honesty to it.

A journalist of Beirut, Joseph Chami, read the verdict of the first "round" of fighting—the first eighteen months—for what it was: The Beirut of "all the Lebanese" had fallen. The old center of the city, the ground of which the various fragments of Beirut met, had been obliterated:

Numbed, Lebanese survivors picked their way mutely through the ruins. The old streets and familiar walls of childhood memory had been disfigured beyond recognition. Gunfire had gouged out the elegant arabesque Ottoman black-and-white inlaid fountains. Shells and missiles had lacerated every dwelling with ugly black-and-blue bullseyes alongside the empty, fire-smudged windows. The souk's honeycomb of rooms and lanes had been smashed by waves of vandals. The old stone dwellings, with their distinctive red-tiled roofs, had crumbled into formless rubble, which spilled into shapeless piles in the streets. A few stone arches were still standing, left upright, by some macabre coincidence, like amputated limbs. Along Bab Edriss, rue George-Picot, and Avenue des Francais, as if a gigantic knife had sliced down from the sky, walls have been sheared off the houses, exposing to view the recesses where Beirut's discreet bourgeoisie in the century before independence had pitched their lives in halftone shades. . . . The old tramline rails which used to snake underfoot in the crowded shopping streets had been cannibalized to serve as girders for the mounds of cobblestone which made such good barricades—after making such good thoroughfares. In the Goldsmith's souk, the base metal of artillery had driven out the precious ingots and smashed the magic workshops. In souk Tawile, holes-in-the-wall were left in the place of the jumble of richly-stocked little shops where generations of Beirut's youngsters had been taken for their annual back-to-school shopping.

Whatever the old world here was really like, men had walked away from it. They had traded its complacency and pretensions, its familiar pains and shortcomings for something entirely different and new. The past would no longer be retrievable: the connection with it had been broken with fury.

The lines drawn by the first year or so of the fighting were to harden. The Maronite world on one side, the Palestinian-led coalition on the other. The reality was there to see. The Palestinian commanders and their semiconventional army had nowhere to go. The turf acquired in Lebanon had become a substitute Palestinian state of sorts. The Palestinian land on the West Bank of the Jordan River was being claimed by Israeli settlers and real estate developers. The commanders of the Palestine Liberation Organization were too old to change their politics, knew no other way. The turf in Lebanon was all they had. No one among the Palestinian leaders stood up and said that the new political turf had replaced the places of the imagination—the cities of Jaffa, Haifa, and Jerusalem that the Palestinians had vowed to liberate. Down the road, at some point in the future, the Palestinians would prevail, it was claimed, they then would bid farewell to the Lebanese who had endured the years of combat and the destruction. Meanwhile business in Lebanon would go on as usual. The incursions into Israel would continue, and so would the Israeli reprisals.

Beirut was not quite home for Yasser Arafat. But it became his capital, seat of his power. No one in Lebanon had the power to dislodge Arafat and his men. The Shia in the south and in Greater Beirut resented the Palestinian dominion, but in a test of arms they could not prevail against the Palestinians. Furthermore the political order in Muslim West Beirut had caved in. The families and notables who had dominated the politics of West Beirut, heirs to a long tradition of power and responsibility, had lost out to the street gangs and the local militias and to the Palestinians. There were several centuries of power behind the Beirut notables. But the gun had prevailed. The Maronites could defend their own turf but were helpless when it came to the Palestinians in the predominantly Muslim parts of the city and the country.

There matters stood until Israel swept into Lebanon in the summer of 1982. A new Israeli cabinet headed by Prime Minister Menachem Begin had finally decided to put an end to the Palestinian sanctuary in Lebanon. (Begin had come to power in 1977, but his second Cabinet, formed in 1981 was a hardline Cabinet with far more radical and militant ideas than the first Begin cycle.) Several things had gone into the making of this new policy. For one, the Maronites in Lebanon, disillusioned with the Syrians who had bailed them out in 1976, had decided to seek Israeli help in the hope of restoring the status quo in the country. There were changes in Israel as well. The revisionist Zionism of Menachem Begin was tougher against the Palestinians than its predecessor Labor Party governments. And in 1981, a new Minister of Defense, General Ariel Sharon was in place ready to try his hand at a major bid to reorder Lebanon's politics. A determined struggle was being waged between Israelis and Palestinians for control of the West Bank of the Jordan River. The new Israeli regime was uncompromising in its determination to assert full and unquestioned Israeli sovereignty over the West Bank. And for a year or two before Israel's invasion of Lebanon, there emerged at the highest reaches of the Israeli government a conviction that the final disposition of the West Bank had to be fought in Lebanon. Smash the Palestinian presence in Lebanon, this line of reasoning had it, and the Palestinian world on the West Bank would submit and accept Israel's terms. Moreover, with the destruction of the Palestine Liberation Organization, Israel would have a chance to prop up a Maronite-based regime in Lebanon to its liking.

Finally there was an American dimension to the making of the Lebanon War of 1982: an American "green light" was given for Israel's invasion of Lebanon. The administration of President Ronald Reagan had vowed toughness against terrorism. Messrs. Begin and Sharon pushed at the limits of America's endorsement and understanding. The war in Lebanon was billed as a war against a major center of terror.

Israel's Lebanon war was an ambitious war with a "grand design." The war broke out on June 6; a week later the Israelis had taken the war to Beirut itself. The city was subjected to a long siege, from mid-June until late August. Its siege became one of the great media stories of recent times. West Beirut was bombarded by land, air, and sea; but the city held on, and displayed a remarkable spirit of defiance. West Beirut held on alone. Early on in the fighting, the Syrians, who had been there since 1976, had beaten a humiliating retreat out of the city. An Israeli commander had sent a message to his Syrian counterpart, a message from "one commander to another," the message read: "We have superior force and shortly we will take over the city. . . . I don't doubt your courage," the Syrian commander was told, but resistance would be "suicidal," the Israeli force was superior in numbers and equipment; the Syrian commander ought to think of the "lives and safety of his men," etc. A map was enclosed, a map specifying the safe roads the Syrians could take out of the besieged city. The Syrians were given a way out and they took it.

In the same vein leaflets were dropped over West Beirut by Israeli planes. "Stop and think," the leaflets warned West Beirut's people: "Think of your safety and the safety of your loved ones, save your life and the lives of your loved ones before it is too late." In these leaflets, too, directions were given for the safe routes out of the besieged city. Some took the exit offered them, the overwhelming majority stayed; it was their home and their city. They had endured seven years of battle; they would wait out the siege. "Stop and Think" became one of the defiant jokes of the besieged city.

An era in Arab politics came to an end with the siege of Beirut: the era that followed the October War of 1973 with all of its hopes, and all the illusions fostered by the new wealth that came to the Arab world with the oil bonanza. The decade that followed the October War had been a time of great hope in the Arab world and of extravagance. The Arabs had become a power in the world, so it was believed. The siege of Beirut served a warrant on these illusions. No one in the Arab world came to the rescue of the embattled city. From the safety of his far away capital in Tripoli, Libya, the militant soldier Muamar al Qaddafi had urged the Palestinian fighters to commit suicide in Beirut and to refuse to quit the city. But Qaddafi had no help to offer, could do nothing for West Beirut and its inhabitants.

In other Arab capitals there was more discretion than in Qaddafi's. But these Arabs too watched Beirut's ordeal as if numbed by the drama. An Arab intellectual of my generation contemplating Beirut's siege put it this way: "I cheered in 1956," he said, remembering the inflated hopes of radical Arab nationalism led by the Egyptian Gamal Abdul Nasser. "I cried in 1967 after the Six Day War. I cheered again in October 1973 when I was told that a new world beckoned the Arabs. Now in the summer of 1982, after a decade that began with such promise closes with a bitter taste of defeat, I am too shocked for words, for tears or even for anger."

Adonis, a brilliant Arab poet, Syrian-born but of Lebanese citizenship, (this is his pen name, his real name is Ali Ahmad Said), who is the most celebrated and gifted writer of this generation, wrote a diary of Beirut under siege in the form of a long poem entitled "The Desert." Here is an excerpt:

My era tells me bluntly:
  You do not belong.
  I answer bluntly:
  I do not belong,
  I try to understand you.
  Now I am a shadow
  Lost in the forest
  Of a skull.

The killing has changed the city's shape—This
            rock
            Is bone
            This smoke people breathing.

We no longer meet,
Rejection and exile keep us apart.
The promises are dead, space is dead,
Death alone has become our meeting point.

A newscast
    About a woman in love
    Being killed,
    About a boy being kidnapped
    And a policeman growing into a wall.

Whatever comes it will be old
        So take with you anything other than this
                madness—get ready
            To stay a stranger . . .

They found people in sacks:
    One without a head
    One without a tongue or hands
    One squashed
    The rest without names.
Have you gone mad? Please,
    Do not write about these things

Darkness.
The earth's trees have become tears on
heaven's cheeks.
An eclipse in this place.
Death snapped the city's branch and the
friends departed.

The flower that tempted the wind to carry its
perfume
        Died yesterday.

The sun no longer rises
It covers its feet with straw
And slips away . . .

Yasser Arafat and his fighters, trapped in the city, played for time, bargained for concessions. Beirut was his Stalingrad, Arafat said. But Menachem Begin was determined to see the fight to the bitter end. Begin wanted Arafat and his men expelled from Lebanon. Under pressure from the Reagan administration to call a halt to Beirut's bombardment, Begin wrote to the American president: "In a war whose purpose is to annihilate the leader of the terrorists in West Beirut, I feel as though I have sent an army to Berlin to wipe out Hitler in his bunker." Beyond Begin's obsessions, the Palestinians had overstayed their welcome in Beirut. In June the population of South Lebanon had greeted the Israeli army with rice and flowers. The people of South Lebanon had endured nearly a decade of Palestinian anarchy and Palestinian power. Entire towns and villages had been seized by the Palestinians, turned into a battleground between Palestinian guerrillas and the Israeli army. The ways of a rural population had been disrupted, and that population had been plunged into an Israeli–Palestinian war beyond their control. Men wanted a return to a normal world, and the invading Israeli army was seen as the best hope of shattering the Palestinian sanctuary, making possible a return to more tranquil times. West Beirut, too, was to break with the Palestinians.

By August, the Beirut establishment—what was left of it—had asked Arafat to quit the city and spare it further carnage. There is a tide in the affairs of men, and it was a time for Arafat and his men to go. As August drew to a close, the Palestinian fighters had evacuated the city: they were dispatched to Syria, to Yemen and South Yemen, to Tunisia, Iraq and Jordan. A multinational force of Americans, French, and Italian soldiers supervised the evacuation. The city (the Muslim western sector of it) gave the Palestinians a grand farewell.

The people of West Beirut had nothing to be ashamed of. If the cause of Palestine was an Arab burden, they had done what they could for the Palestinians. They had given the Palestinian armed presence a decade. Moreover, they had done it at a time when there was peace between Egypt and Israel, and a great economic boom in the Arab oil states. Beirut had never occupied the place in Arab and Muslim history that the great cities of Cairo and Damascus and Baghdad had, but in the summer of 1982, the city never known for serious political undertakings, suffered for a large Arab cause. And the Arab world had been a spectator to the terrible ordeal of the summer of 1982.

Israel's first objective—the expulsion of the Palestinians—had been easy to achieve. But the new order Israel sought to build under its tutelage was not to be. Israel's hope had rested on a young Maronite, Basheer Gemayyel, the younger of the two sons of the leader of the Phalange Party. Basheer Gemayyel was thirty-four years old when Israel helped secure his election to the Presidency in August of 1982. He had risen through the world of the militias; he was "tough" and was admired for it. He had secured control over the Maronite world and had shown no mercy doing it; he had a good deal of blood on his hands. He was an impatient young man who was convinced that the old Lebanese republic of compromise had issued in ruin. Basheer Gemayyel wanted a strong state, saw himself as the leader of a new generation that would break with the ways and the world of the country's elders.

Basheer Gemayyel was elected on August 23. On September 14, President-elect Basheer Gemayyel was dug out of the rubble of the Phalange headquarters in East Beirut. He had gone there, as was his habit on every Tuesday afternoon, to attend a meeting of the party. A blast, activated by remote control, shattered the three-story building. It was a brief Maronite and Lebanese dream: the young finding a way out of the abyss into which the country had fallen. It was also the end of the Israeli design.

This had been Israel's first war of choice. And a grim massacre carried out by Basheer Gemayyel's men in the

Palestinian refugee camps of West Beirut—a massacre that occurred after the Israeli armed forces escorted Basheer Gemayyel's men to the camps—drove home to the Israeli public the costs and follies of Israel's venture into Lebanon. The facts of the massacre were laid bare by an Israeli commission of inquiry headed by Yitzhak Kahan, president of the Supreme Court. On Thursday, September 16, two days after Basheer Gemayyel's assassination, a unit of his followers made up of approximately 150 men made its way to the Palestinian refugee camps. Hitherto, the Phalangists had resisted Israel's repeated requests to enter into Muslim West Beirut. But Basheer's death had to be avenged; hence the entry into the Palestinian camps. The Israeli army provided illumination for the entering forces "intermittently throughout the night," the Kahan Commission of Inquiry states. The Phalangist unit stayed in the camps until the morning of Saturday, September 18. Hundreds of men and women and children were murdered. "No prophetic powers," the Kahan Commission report stated "were required to know that concrete dangers of slaughter existed." The "direct respon-sibility," the Commission concluded, was that of the unit that entered the camps; but the "indirect responsibility" was to be borne by Israel's chain of command. The entry into the camps was presented as an effort to root out two thousand armed men remaining there. No such force had been left in the camps. In a way, though, the logic of the massacres was the logic of the entire war. So elusive was the war's aim—a war against Palestinian nationalism—that it was easier to launch than to conclude. There was always another hill around the corner and another Palestinian.

The Israeli bid had been blunted. Israel did not know the country, did not understand its passions and feuds, could not be a legitimate party to its politics. Israel could not turn demography around, shore up a Maronite hegemony in a land that was becoming increasingly Muslim in numbers. And soon,

rather like the Palestine Liberation Organization before it, Israel would wear out its welcome, turn against its presence in Lebanon those who had viewed with great relief the arrival of its armor in June of 1982.

It was America's turn as redeemer after September 1982. And America was the kind of redeemer that the Lebanese dreamt of. Here was a distant great power, one with great cultural appeal and allure taking an interest in Lebanon. There had always been a propensity among the Lebanese to think that their small country mattered to the "masters of the world," that the mighty cared about Lebanon's fate. The arrival in Lebanon in September of a "multinational peace force" made up of U.S., French, Italian, and British units played into Lebanon's myths; the force, a symbolic contingent of five thousand men, had come under American auspices. A great, wealthy power had committed itself to Lebanon's salvation; there was no need for the Lebanese to live in the shadow of either Israel or Syria.

This was a great misunderstanding: a hasty decision for the superpower from afar, a great event in the life of a small, fractured republic with a vivid imagination, with accounts to be settled, with the hatreds of a violent decade still playing themselves out. The affair began with promise; it ended in tragedy for the Lebanese and for the power from afar.

The American commitment was open-ended and ambigu-ous, primarily motivated by guilt: guilt for the "green light" given Israel's invasion and for the massacres in the Palestinian camps. The hope was that America would give the regime of President Amin Gemayyel—Amin had been elected to the Presidency after the assassination of his younger brother—a chance.

This was another case of American innocence abroad. The U.S. had once again stepped into a foreign land unaware of that land's memories and grievances. And in due time, the petty privileges and feuds of one sect in an alien society were to become part of America's prestige and "credibility" and national honor.

America had indulged hopes beyond her imagination. And for a brief moment, from the fall of 1982 until the fall a year later, there was in Lebanon the heady sense of a "new order" in the making. The gifted *New York Times* reporter, Thomas Friedman, who covered this period in Lebanon with great artistry and depth wrote of these hopes in a dispatch of November 1, 1982. For the friends of America, for the Maronite Christians and the few Muslim notables who placed their faith in American power, an "unabashedly pro-American era" had begun. And the political order they had in mind was to be "aloof from the currents of Arab nationalism and governed by a conservative alliance dominated by Maronite Christians but also including Muslim privileged classes." Mr. Friedman quoted one of the country's most articulate men, Ghassan Tueni, American-educated, a publisher of Beirut's leading paper *An Nahar*, a man who represented the country at the United Nations: "The Che Guevara era of Lebanese politics is over. People here have had their fling with radicalism. Beards and jeans are out now. Neckties are in." But around the corner, there was a more ferocious radicalism than yesterday's.

The new order pushed on against the Druze and the Shia at home, and against Syrian power and influence. Behind the shield and prestige of a great power the Maronite regime of Amin Gemayyel had set out to subdue an unwieldy country. In the scheme of this narrowly based regime, the Druze in the Shuf mountains were to be subdued, and the vast Shia population in Greater Beirut to be "thinned out," with large numbers of squatters cleared out, sent back to their ancestral land in the South and the Bekaa Valley. But the new order rested on weak foundations. In the same dispatch on the illusions of the pro-America era, Mr. Friedman wrote about Ali Halloum, fifty years of age, a father of ten, a Shia from the southern slums of the city. Ali Halloum had been expelled from his old home in northeast Beirut; that neighborhood had fallen to the Maronite militias. He now lived in a squatter settlement that the government wanted to bulldoze: "We came here," Ali Halloum said, "from East Beirut during the civil war. When we arrived it was all sand dunes. . . . There is an Armenian living in my house in East Beirut. Give me my house back and I will give you this one. I am telling you either they give me somewhere else to live or I die in my house."

Ali Halloum's new house was close to Beirut's international airport, close to the U.S. Marine headquarters. The southern slums of the city had become a vast urban sprawl. Hooterville was the name given this neighborhood by the Marines. The U.S. Marines lived in close proximity to deadly passions and fears. They were placed in harm's way. In military jargon, their location was a "permissive" environment hard to seal off and to protect. But they had been placed here, close to the airport, to convey normalcy, to show the flag, to show that Lebanon was on the mend. The "rules of engagement" given the Marines were rules of innocence, of a "peacekeeping force." "Do not chamber a round," the rules of engagement specified, "unless told so by a commissioned officer unless you must act in self-defense where deadly force is authorized. . . . Call local forces (Lebanese Armed Forces) to assist in self-defense effort. Notify headquarters. Use only minimum degree of force to accomplish any mission. . . . Protect innocent civilians from harm."

At first the neighborhood was friendly to the Marines. In *The Root*, a book by Marine historian Eric Hammel, narrated for the most part in the words of the men who had served in Lebanon, we read that, if anything, the civilians were "embarrassingly cordial." But that, too, would change. There were the embittered claimants in "Hooterville"; there was a clumsy and cruel Phalange regime starting battles it could not conclude, settling old accounts only to give rise to new resentments. And there were two powers, Syria and Iran, determined to push the Americans out of Lebanon, to put an end to the pro-American era and to the reign of America's clients.

On April 18, 1983 a car bomb shattered the American embassy in Beirut killing sixty-three people. And in "Hooter-ville," the Marines reported seeing new and large portraits of America's Iranian nemesis, Ayatollah Ruhollah Khomeini. The American presence had become a source of trouble. America did not have enough presence in Lebanon to prevail. What American power was deployed in Lebanon was enough to tempt the Maronites and embitter their Druze and Shia rivals. And it was enough to provide the pied piper of the Muslim poor, Ayatollah Ruhollah Khomeini in Iran, with a convenient American target in an exposed place. The Iranian revolution was reluctant to take on American power in the Gulf. But Iran was now, thanks to its ties to the Shia of Lebanon, a power in the Mediterranean.

There were minor skirmishes between the Marines and snipers from the southern slums in the summer of '83. By September the flotilla of American warships off the coast of Lebanon was shelling the hills in the Shuf mountains, southeast of the city. The entire spectacle had a surrealistic quality: the warships could not win, could not make the Druze and the Shia accept a hostile regime; but the distant power did not know how to quit, could not write off its entire venture and admit that it had misread the reality of an alien place. Much has been written about the American expedition to Lebanon, about the warships shelling the hills overlooking Beirut. But nothing can match a passage in Joseph Conrad's *Heart of Darkness* where Marlow, Conrad's narrator, is telling of the strange thing he witnessed on a French steamer on his way deep into wilderness:

Once, I remember, we came upon a man-of-war anchored off the coast. There wasn't even a shed there,

and she was shelling the bush. . . . In the empty immensity of earth, sky, and water, there she was, incomprehensible, firing into a continent. Pop, would go one of the six-inch guns; a small flame would dart and vanish, a little white smoke would disappear, a tiny projectile would give a feeble screech—and nothing happened. Nothing could happen. There was a touch of insanity in the proceeding, a sense of lugubrious drollery in the sight; and it was not dissipated by somebody on board assuring me earnestly there was a camp of natives—he called them enemies!—hidden out of sight somewhere.

But we live in a more deadly world than Marlow's: On the morning of October 23, a young driver in a Mercedes truck loaded with TNT blew up the Marines' headquarters. The blast shattered all eight floors of the building. This is from Thomas Friedman's dispatch to *The New York Times*: "Some Marines said that the presence of mind of the driver who steered the truck through all the barriers, swerved around bunkers, ignored the rifle fire directed at him and then detonated a bomb not a moment too soon was nothing short of remarkable." Two hundred and forty-one U.S. Servicemen were killed.

Two minutes later, a similar explosion destroyed the French barracks. This was a smaller explosion. Fifty-eight of France's troops were killed. Sentiment, one French observer said, had brought the French to Lebanon, an old sense of mission.

There was no American interest in Lebanon, and there was no use pretending. An American president who vowed to "stand tall" against terrorism was unable to make a clean break. But the countdown for American withdrawal had begun. And on January 18, 1984 a crime took place in Beirut which delivered its own verdict on the despair of the city, on its break with its past. Malcolm Kerr, the president of the American University of Beirut, was murdered as he made his way to his office. Kerr, fifty-two years of age, was born in Beirut to a family of missionaries, with long ties to the Arab world and to the university. He was born in the same hospital where he was pronounced dead. His father, Stanley Kerr, had been professor of biochemistry at the university, his mother had served as dean of women. American Protestant missionaries and teachers like Kerr's parents had a tradition of philanthropy and service in Beirut which stretched back to the 1820s. In 1866, American missionaries and philanthropists had established the university: its first name was the Syrian Protestant College. Generations of Americans had come to the AUB to teach. And Kerr, with a brilliant and secure career at the University of California at Los Angeles, had gone back to Lebanon in the aftermath of the war of 1982 to do what he could for the university.

Like the city, the university itself had been divided. There was its campus on the western coastline, but this was on Muslim grounds now. A new branch of the university had opened in East Beirut to serve the Christian students and faculty. The American inheritance had been claimed by the two combatants; and before his murder, Malcolm Kerr had walked a tightrope, doing what he could for the university, lobbying the U.S. for financial support and trying to insulate the university, to the extent possible, from the violence and political claims of the city. It was no secret that in East Beirut the Phalange viewed Kerr with suspicion, that they did not see him as their kind of American. And it was known as well that there were conspirators and true believers in Muslim West Beirut determined to make the place fully theirs, to banish from their part of the city all those who embodied and represented the power and the message of America.

Malcolm Kerr, a brilliant Arabist and student of Islam, had no illusion about the politics of the Arab world or of Lebanon. Even a decade earlier, he had glimpsed the passing of an old Arab world and the bare outlines of a more cruel one. The "fun," he said, had gone out of Arab politics after the Arab defeat of 1967. "In the good old days," he added, "Arabs refused to take themselves seriously and this made it easy to take a relaxed view of the few who possessed intimations of some immortal mission." He had written this in 1970. And in an essay written in 1981 he depicted the landscape of Arab politics with remarkable brevity and power; he linked the spectacle of killing in Lebanon and the display of wealth in the Arab oil states. These were "joint ventures" he said, "the scandalous expenditure of many billions of dollars each year on useless construction projects in Saudi Arabia, and the unceasing orgy of killing and destruction in Lebanon." These were the twin hallmarks of the new Arab world: "It is noteworthy that these two operations are both 'joint ventures' in which the Arab world as a whole participates, collaboratively in one case, combatively in the other; and in both cases parties in the outside world are major participants also, fellow builders, as it were, of the new Arab order." Kerr knew the risks; but it had been his childhood dream to preside over the university. The tall boyish-looking Arabist had returned to a monstrous city.

The Reagan Administration still talked of not "walking away" from a difficult situation. In early February, its spokesmen were insisting that "the forces of radicalism and extremism" will not be allowed to prevail in Lebanon. But on February 6, when the combined forces of the Shia and the Druze took over West Beirut in an open defiance of the Maronite-based regime, America made the final decision to quit Lebanon. America had been training units of the Lebanese army. Young Lebanese recruits had done an adequate job mimicking the Marines down to the Marines' marching chants, and the "high and tight" haircuts. But the Lebanese army had just melted away, split along sectarian lines. All along the army had a Muslim Shia rank-and-file majority. And the simple countryside boys had refused to do battle in defense of that pro-American era. The American presence had become untenable. The Marines were "deployed" to the ships, it was announced. The American warships pounded the hills: the retreat was to be covered up by a demonstration of American might.

For America's clients, it was a time of great disillusion. The distant power, the clients said, had not been "tough enough," had only been a "spectator." In a city hardened by all it had seen, the clients of America spun the following satirical tale:

A man curious about the battleship *New Jersey* which was shelling the hills took a rowboat out to look at the ship. And there, in the Mediterranean, the curious man saw why America had not been able to tame the rabble: the battleship was a cardboard cut-out. Redemption was promised, and it was not to be. The Lebanese were on their own again.

And there was in the country a new bid for power: a Shia bid. The country had new inheritors. Disorganized, clamouring to be heard, geographically dispersed in three locations—the Bekaa Valley in the east, Greater Beirut, the south—the force of Shia numbers and their passion could not be denied. Their leaders in Beirut, only yesterday strangers to the politics of the city, and marginal men, had defended the place of the urban Shia. The large southern suburbs which were their stronghold—home to a population of 700,000, perhaps more—were there to stay. Meanwhile, in the south, Israel's occupation had served as the midwife of a militant Shia movement led by uncompromising clerics, determined to push Israel out of South Lebanon. There too suicide drivers had struck Israeli installations and waged a relentless struggle against Israel. The fight against Israel had given the Shia a new sense of self-confidence. In the Bekaa Valley Shia extremists held sway. To the Bekaa, through Syria, had come Iranian revolutionary guardsmen, clerical guides, Iranian support. Iran had its clerical state, its armed mullahs, its Party of God, its militant young men willing to die in pursuit of a "reign of virtue." The symbols and rituals of Shiism, once invitations to submission, had been reinterpreted, turned to an ethos of martyrdom and zeal.

Moreover, the Shia of Lebanon had a great religious drama of their own. In the summer of 1978, their beloved Iranian-born leader Musa al Sadr had vanished in Libya. He had gone there to visit Libya's leader Muamar al Qaddafi and was never heard from again. Musa al Sadr had reenacted his people's sacred drama of an Imam who disappears and is destined to return and bring about a reign of justice. Musa al Sadr had commanded power when he was amongst his followers, but his absence turned him into a great cult figure. Hard-headed men were sure that he had been murdered by Qaddafi, but the myth had a power that defied all hard-headed explanations.

In Musa al Sadr the unwashed had a prophet, and in Iran they had the inspiration of a people released from old fears. The Shia had arrived, or so it seemed. But the inheritors celebrating their triumph in a city they once viewed with awe were laying claim to ruins. When it worked, and when it was precious, the city had belonged to different kinds of men and women: men and women with polish, at ease in the world of foreigners, men and women with security and pedigree. The new claimants had their passion, their old resentments, and they had the gospel of radicalized religion. Complacency—the complacency of a time not so long ago—had yielded to the politics of wrath. The small pockets of affluence and privilege and polish had stood perilously close to crowded alleyways where the multitudes watched and resented. Then one day privilege found itself helpless: It was left mourning for yesterday's grace, remembering better times. The new claimants couldn't share this sorrow—it was a different city that they remembered.

No one could really "win" in Beirut. In the mid-1970s, the combatants fought over beachfront hotels, over once-proud places. A decade later they were fighting over shells of gutted buildings. Men being what they are, the shells of buildings had to be called "strategic." With great zeal the warring factions were busy blowing up the ground on which they themselves stood. Violence, a young Lebanese scholar, Farid el Khazen wrote in a letter from Beirut, had become random with "no identifiable target, no return address." Violence aimed "neither at deposing a government nor at publicizing specific concerns." The social and economic grievances which had helped spark the war and give it its ferocity had been overwhelmed. Those grievances could not be addressed, there was no state to dispense justice, no standing political and economic order that would atone for past sins.

At some early point in the war, men must have believed that out of the ruins of a compromised and unjust city a better one would emerge, that after the work of destruction is done men would build something more viable. In the fantasy, where a city of cultural mimicry once stood, there would rise an authentic city with a clear vocation, a city with a cultural message of its own, a city that was not for hire—a city without a brothel in its center, a place where the pampered classes would not permit themselves such liberties and prerogatives. Such a fantasy must have been at work among the Muslim militias, among the leftist parties and those who believed that the war would give them a chance to build a better society. The Maronite Christians must have had ideas of their own. The country's sovereignty would be defended, the meddling of Arab states, of Palestinians, in its affairs would be put to an end. Before his assassination, in 1982, Basheer Gemayyel had talked of a country that would not be a "farm" or a "bridge" for others to cross, or a place of compromise; he had talked of an "orderly" place that would work, of a more principled society. But out of the killing and the waste, out of the passions and the feud, the Lebanese had come out empty-handed. Beirut couldn't be the site for a great movement of redemption, couldn't be made pure or self-sufficient, and its people still had their age-old habit of calling on outsiders, on foreign powers, to help them vanquish a neighbor nearby.

So much had slipped away. There remained the feud with other men, and in a ruined place the feud was a precious possession. The feud with other men, with other clans, within the same family at that, had always been passionate here, clung to and remembered. The scarcity, the hard economic and psychic boundaries of the place, the scramble of men caught in a world so severely hemmed in by tradition and poverty, gave the feud great ferocity and power. Now the feud was exalted, given ideological covers of all sorts.

No one could be sure of anything: "alliances" were like tales of the Thousand and One Nights, tales of treachery and intrigue. Back in 1984 Druze and Shia battled Maronites, as "brothers" they were then. Less than two years later, the Shia and the Druze were tearing at each other, battling for supremacy over the alleys of West Beirut. Maronites had hated Palestinians with a vengeance, and had seen them as "strangers" defiling a beloved homeland. They had fought them for more than a decade. To banish the Palestinians from Lebanon, the Maronites had made common cause with the Syrians, with the Israelis, and then the Americans. By 1986 there was a Palestinian-Maronite entente. The common enemy of the Palestinians and the Maronites had become the Shia and the Syrian regime of Hafez Assad.

Men had drawn lines. The enemies were supposed to be on the other side of the line. But there were feuds amongst men who partook of the same faith. The bloodletting in East Beirut among different factions in the Maronite world was not about faith and embattled Christianity. Faith was only a mask. And faith was also a mask in the Shia world, where Party of God extremists battled Amal (meaning "hope"), the Shia militia that the absent Musa al Sadr had put together back in 1975. Amal represented the mainstream of Shia Lebanon, and its members wanted for their sect pride of place in Lebanon's sectarian political game. The men of Amal were not religiously zealous or particularly ideological; they wanted the spoils of power and a marginal change in the way the country was governed. The majority of the true believers of the Party of God were young men who had grown up in the ruined alleyways of Beirut's southern suburbs. They knew the southern slums and the streets of Muslim West Beirut. Of that Maronite society beyond the line, they knew practically nothing. The militiamen lobbed shells into East Beirut; they knew that Maronite society was a hostile one. But they had not experienced life in the Maronite towns of Mount Lebanon, nor did they appreciate the depth of Maronite history or the power of the Maronite church and the determination of the Maronites to keep their world intact. That kind of knowledge would have required exposure to the Maronites, but the long war had diminished everyone's world.

They were sons of peasants, the young men in the southern Shia slums of Beirut who found in radicalized Islam the answers to their distress. Their connection to the land, to their ancestral villages, had been broken. For them there was no way back to the certainty of the land, to the simple village ways. They knew the tales of these villages: the tales had been transmitted to them by parents, by village elders and raconteurs. And memory had made of these villages pretty places of the imagination. Left alone, left undisturbed by wars and invasions and "movements of national liberation," the village life would have eroded. These villages in the hinterland of the country had no way of feeding their people or sustaining their ambitions. Men would have walked away from the village ways when they were ready to do so. There would have been much less grief and yearning for the past. But men had been banished before they were ready. And they were banished when there was no alternative world to inherit. In their own view of things, these men denied a past, saw things with clarity: they had possessed a world and outsiders had made that world brutal and unwelcoming.

The functionaries and mullahs and young men who comprised the Party of God drew their inspiration from Iran and saw themselves as an extension of the Iranian revolution further east. In the difficult place which was Lebanon, the Party of God zealots said that they were committed to the establishment of an "Islamic Republic." In a document issued in February 1985, the Party of God urged Lebanon's Christians to convert to Islam. "Oh Christians we call you to Islam; in it you will find your safety and happiness, the rewards in this life and in the hereafter." The new Shia millenarians looked past the country's religious division, its seventeen sects, its cramped neighborhoods, its location in the shadow of Israel and Syria, its harsh economic limits. Newly urbanized, the young believers of the Party of God were pushed on by a sense of messianic fulfillment. In a far-away Iranian state they knew so little about, they had their Imam, their saviour and leader. The faraway Iranian realm was a vast state with oil, with territory, with a large population. But Lebanon's true believers insisted that Iran's theocracy knew no boundaries, that they too were part of the Imam's realm.

It was of Islam that the Party of God believers spoke. In their fantasy Islam was pure and the Islamic community, the Islamic *Umma*, was one. But in reality there was that deep schism between Sunni, orthodox Islam and the Shia revolution of Iran and its ideological off-shoots in the Arab world. The Sunnis of Lebanon could only see the Party of God utopia as the rallying cry of an aggrieved sect. In earlier times, the Sunnis of Lebanon had been the standard-bearers of Islam in Lebanon, and the coastal cities of Lebanon, West Beirut included, had been theirs. The rise of "the oppressed of the earth" that Ayatollah Khomeini and his Lebanese devotees preached was anathema to the Sunnis of Lebanon. What the Party of God believers saw as Islam's truth and Islam's call, the merchant communities of Sunni West Beirut could only see as the intrusion of Iran and its radical message into their world.

A terrible wind was blowing throughout the world of Islam—an aggrieved nativist movement. The middle ground of Muslim modernism had collapsed: It was wrath on one side, privilege on the other. It was revolutionary Iran pitted against the Sunni-ruled states in the Gulf. The messiah of the Iranian revolution, Ayatollah Khomeini, had summoned men to rebellion. He had rallied under his banner the excluded in Arab politics. A large, historic fight had broken out between the Iranian revolution and the dominant political order in the Arab world. It was the rebels against those who had acquired earthly political kingdoms, the children of the millennium against the settled classes. This was a clash of two rival historical temperaments: the angry, unreconciled excluded on one side, the smug self-assured on the other, the "saints" versus the merchants. This large fight over the soul and direction of modern Muslim society was fought out in Beirut as it was being waged further east between Iraq and Iran. In the ruined city by the Mediterranean, the Iranians had found fertile soil for their brand of messianic politics. Here was a city where Western hostages could be held on Iran's behalf and traded for weapons and political concessions while still maintaining the fiction of Iran's innocence.

In the new politics of the city, there was a thin line between ideology and banditry. Men began as ideologues, or so they said, and ended up as bandits. It happened to the Palestinians, and among the Maronites, then among the Shia. The politics of the city, and that of the country at large, had become the realm of warlords and bandits. This being a style-conscious city, the bandits were men of flair. There was a young Druze bandit named "the cowboy": he went around the turf over which he presided with a cowboy hat, bodyguards, and swagger. There was a Kurdish bandit, called Abu Abdu the Kurd, nick-named the Electronic Man. He had been shot in the throat, and he spoke through some electronic device installed in his throat. There was another bandit called "Saif al Dahia," "the sword of

the southern suburbs." The Party of God lieutenants went around the city in BMWs; those of the Amal movement in Volvos. A ransacked house had graffiti scribbled on a wall: "Rambo was here." Everything was a legitimate item for commerce: drugs, hashish, guns, Western hostages.

At the apex of the country's politics there was a mix of sons of old families, and of men of more modest background who had ridden the chaos and the disorder to new-found power and influence. The warlords, both the old variety and the upstarts, offered the country nothing new. Indeed their ways only guaranteed a perpetuation of the nightmare. But they were obeyed and admired by their communities all the same. The warlords strutted like peacocks among the ruins. Young starry-eyed boys trailed them, ready to die for them. The warlords were men with no regrets. Something a French consul-general, Joseph Couget, said of Lebanese leaders more than seventy years ago applies to the men who now share power over Lebanon's fragments. "The feeling of devotion to the little native country (patrie)," he wrote in a memorandum in 1913, "does not exist among Lebanese officials and everyone of them is always ready, according to a well-known expression, to set his country on fire in order to light his cigarette."

The warlords had their turfs and their feuds and their bravado. But the country had been stripped of what little independence it possessed. In the southern part of the country, Israel had what it called its "security zone," a strip of land controlled by an army of mercenaries that Israel sustained and paid for. The "South Lebanon Army" had been led by a renegade Lebanese officer, Maj. Saad Haddad, who had answered to Israel and relied upon its power. After his death in 1984, Israel had found another Lebanese army officer, this time a retired general by the name of Antoine Lahd, and the general picked up where his predecessor left off. The South Lebanon Army—a predominantly Christian force—patrolled the strip of land which it exalted as "Free Lebanon." The Israeli quest for hegemony over Lebanon had played itself out by 1983 and had been blunted by the Syrians. Of that short-lived dream which the architects of Israel's war venture into Lebanon had in mind, there remained that strip of land which bordered Israel, and a dependent mercenary army. In the rest of the country, there was the lengthening shadow of Syria.

In late February of 1987 a Syrian expedition of 7,000 soldiers entered Muslim West Beirut. The Syrians came at the invitation of some of Lebanon's dominant Muslim figures. The country's prime minister, a patrician from the Muslim Sunni city of Tripoli, the country's minister of justice and head of the Shia mainstream movement, another Shia notable who occupied the post of speaker of parliament, and the old establishment of the city of Beirut gave their blessing to the Syrian entry to Beirut.

The chaos of Muslim West Beirut knew no limit. For nearly two years the Syrians' Shia allies had been doing battle against the Palestinian refugee camps. The "war of the camps" had stalled. From Tunis, his base of operations, Yasser Arafat and the exiled leaders of the Palestine Liberation Organization, had channeled money and weapons and men to the refugee camps in Lebanon. The refugee camps, disarmed in 1982, had again been turned into armed fortresses, an explicit defiance of Syria's wishes. The extremism of the Iranian sponsored Party of God, too, troubled the Syrians. In alliance, the Syrians and the Iranians had pushed the Americans out of Lebanon. But the Syrians and the Iranians had in mind different ideas for the country. And the Syrians came in February to assert that they were the dominant foreign power in Lebanon. A circle was closed: the Syrians had been in Beirut before; they had come in 1976 and had not been able to prevent the chaos. This time the Syrians were quick to announce a new regime for the city. Twenty-three members of the Party of God were lined up against a wall and killed right after the arrival of the Syrian

forces. The city had seen too much carnage to be really awed by this display of cruelty.

In a different era, the arrival of the Syrians into West Beirut would have been seen as the fall of a city of grace and liberties to a conquering army of a brutal regime nearby. But nothing of the kind was said. An army from an orderly capital that worked had been dispatched to a city that played with fire.

Beirut's political story offered nothing new: neither the local warlords nor the foreign armies could restore its truth. Nizzar Qabbani, a poet of Beirut, one of the Arab world's outstanding poets (he was actually born in Syria, but he lived and wrote his poetry in Beirut, and that too was part of the old culture of the city) offered Beirut an elegy of sorrow. He cut through the political claims to say some poignant words about the fate of the city. Qabbani had lost his wife in one of Beirut's countless episodes of violence (a bombing, in 1981, of the Iraqi embassy); he had known the city's charms, and he had been victimized by its cruelty. Beirut, he said, is a "ball of fire that has burned my hands. But I still hold onto it," just like the child who puts in the palm of his hands "poisonous insects, who holds onto a scorpion without being afraid of being stung." The Beirut of the 1950s and '60s—the enchanted city of his youth where he wrote daring poetry about sex and romance, the city of poetry and pleasures—is a "thing of the past." You can't bring it back to life as you can't bring back the "old glories of Rome and Athens":

> History is a river that never flows backward. . . . We must have the courage to admit that the war in Lebanon has overturned the old Lebanon. Some of us may dream of young Beirut, of the playful city that enthralled millions of men, but we must be realistic and consider the city before us. Nothing remains of old Beirut except the scent of it that blows from old notebooks. . . .

1. A young man with a gift given him by his hero Basheer Gemayyel.

2. Arriving in Junieh.

3. The waterfront of Junieh.

4. Palestinian demonstration in the Beddawi refugee camp.

5. An elderly Druze in traditional attire.

6. A Christian wedding in East Beirut.

7. Beddawi refugee camp, Tripoli.

8. Shia militiamen: time out for prayer.

9. In the southern town of Nabatiye following a religious festival.

10. "Martyrs'" posters in Beirut's southern suburbs.*
    (Please refer to Notes for pictures marked with an asterisk.)

11. The Maronite Patriarch, Mar Nasrallah Butrus Sufayr, and a visiting politician.*

12. School children, Tripoli in background.

13. A Christian family on a picnic in Junieh.

14. Lebanese soldiers, an African student.

15. At a Christian wedding in East Beirut.

16. An Ethiopian woman.

17. A "lady of the evening," East Beirut.

18. In the streets of Beddawi camp.

19. An art festival on the eastern side of Beirut's green line.

20. A Druze woman in al Shuwayfat, a suburb of Beirut.

21. Outside a mosque in the southern suburbs.

22. Palestinian fighters, Tripoli.

23. Evacuating Beddawi refugee camp.

24. In the town of Suq al Gharb, a shopkeeper leaving his shop behind.*

25. Shia women of the southern suburbs.

26. U.S. Marines digging foxholes on the outskirts of the southern suburbs.

27. Next to Our Lady of Lebanon, Lady Harissa, a cathedral.

28. After a break, Palestinian fighters.

29. Mother in mourning, East Beirut.

30. Shelling in West Beirut during heavy fighting in 1984.

31. The seaside near Junieh.*

32. The Palestinian refugee camps of Sabra and Shatila.

33. An amusement park in West Beirut.

34. A christening in East Beirut.

35. Palestinian in the Beddawi refugee camp.

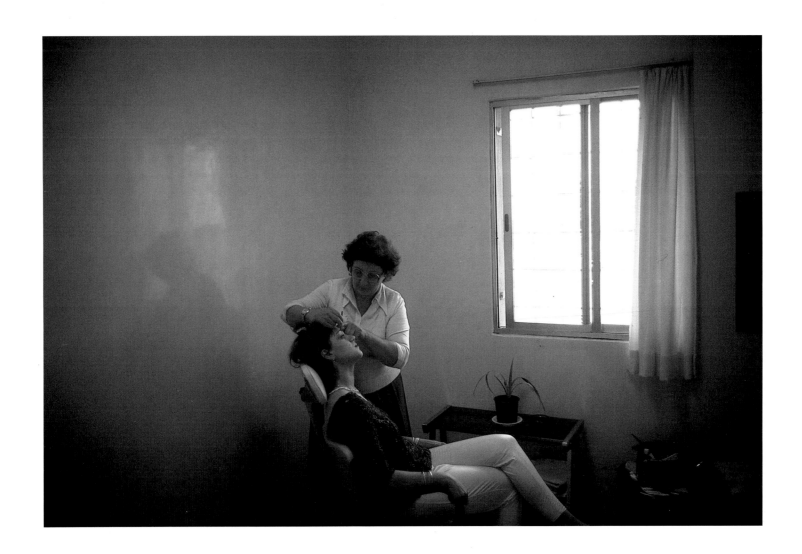

36. Beauty parlor.

37. Guard duty, Maronite militia.

38. Palestinian family, Tripoli.

39. The apartment of a Druze family in Aley.

40. A wedding in East Beirut.

41. Evacuation from West Beirut by an
    American helicopter.

42. Country club in the Junieh area.

43. A Marine sentry at the U.S. Embassy.

44. A father and his son after the son's christening.

45. A street during the lull in the fighting.

46. A street in Beirut's southern suburbs.*

47. In the Palestinian refugee camp of Beddawi near Tripoli, man and young fighter walk the streets.

48. A cobbler in the southern suburbs.

49. The hospital in Aley after shelling by U.S. battleships.

50. In the Nahr al Barid refugee camp during Palestinian in-fighting an old man bemoans the fighting.

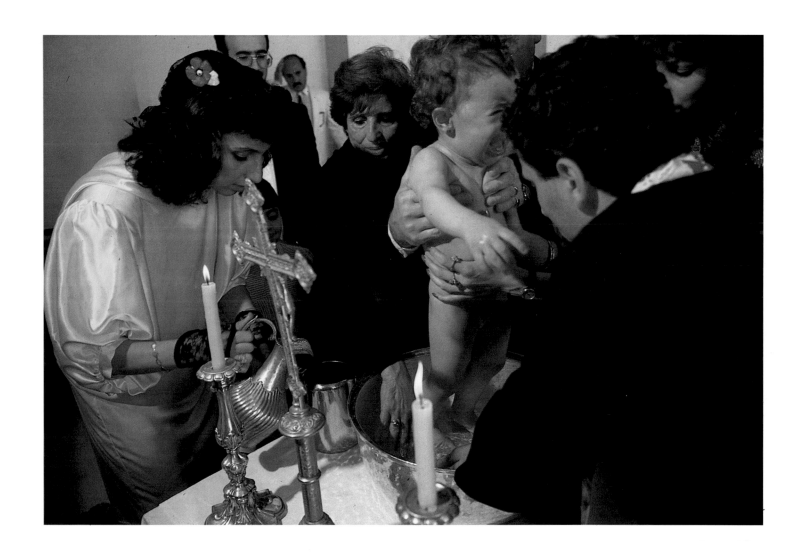

51. Christening, East Beirut.

52. Maronite priest at the Maronite university of Kaslik.*

53. The day after Palestinian fighting in Nahr al Barid refugee camp.

54. Wounded man with family, Tripoli.

55. A corpse on Tripoli's street. The morgue and refrigerator trucks were full.

56. Visitors to the statue of Our Lady of Lebanon.*

57. Weapons in a Christian village.

58. Boys in the southern suburbs playing at war.

59. A bomb shelter during the shelling of an apartment building.

60. A Palestinian fighter, Beddawi area.

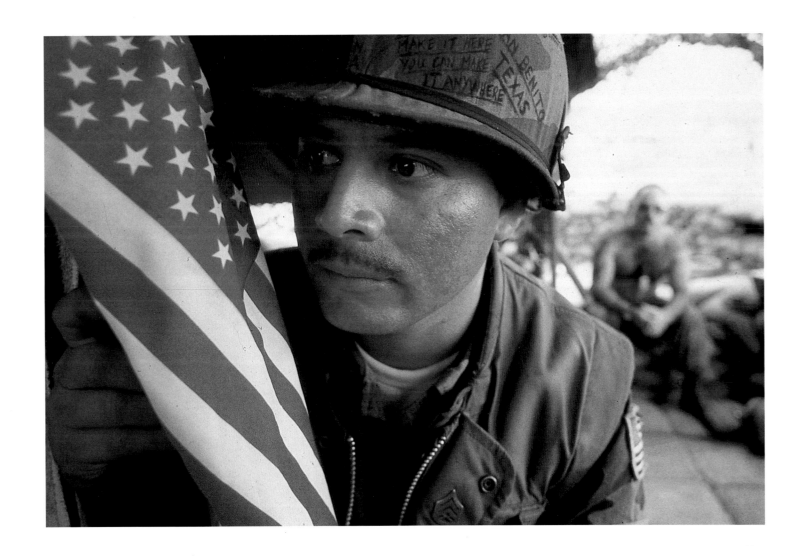

61. Newly arrived U.S. Marines.

62. A shrapnel-scarred building in West Beirut.

63. "B" girl in a West Beirut bar.

64. Beauty queen, Miss Lebanon (right) and her mother.

65. Christian Lebanese fire from East Beirut green line into West Beirut.

66. An orphaned boy with part of a weapon.

67. Shia women.

68. Family reunion, mountain village.*

69. A U.S. Marine in a helicopter.

70. Homeless people in Tripoli waiting for bedding and clothing.

71. East Beirut restaurant.

72. Maronite church near Junieh.

73. U.S. Marines under fire preparing for evacuation.

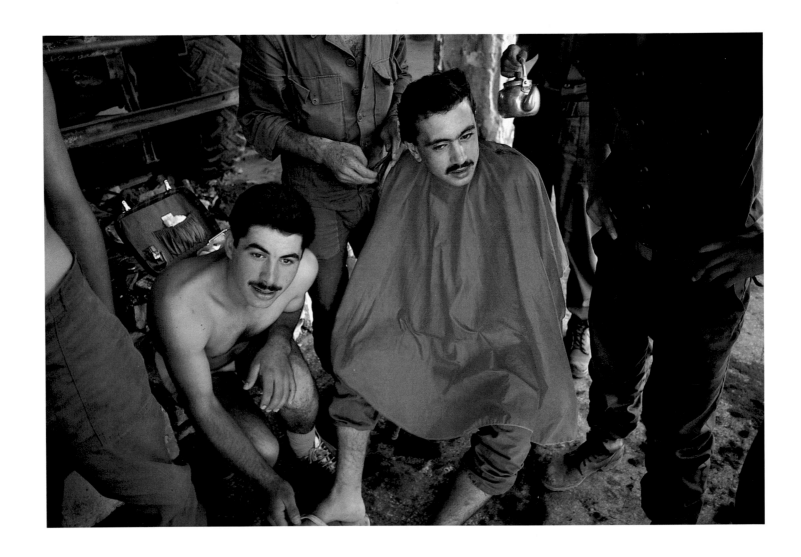

74. Lebanese army soldiers.

75. Marine checkpoint near the American Embassy.

76. A seaside view in West Beirut.

77. Returning from the beach in East Beirut near Junieh.

78. A Shia mosque in the southern suburbs.

79. Young girls in Junieh.

80. Young Shia women in Beirut's southern suburbs.*

81. Rehabilitation center in East Beirut mountains.

82. An amusement park in West Beirut.

83. Druze checkpoint near the West Beirut amusement park.

84. Seaside boulevard in West Beirut.

85. Running for cover in the southern suburbs.

86. In the Palestinian refugee camps of Sabra and Shatila.

87. Palestinian fighter north of Tripoli.

88. Waiting for shelling to subside while moving about Beddawi camp.

89. Visitors near Suq al Gharb.

90. Two Marines on Beirut's outskirts.

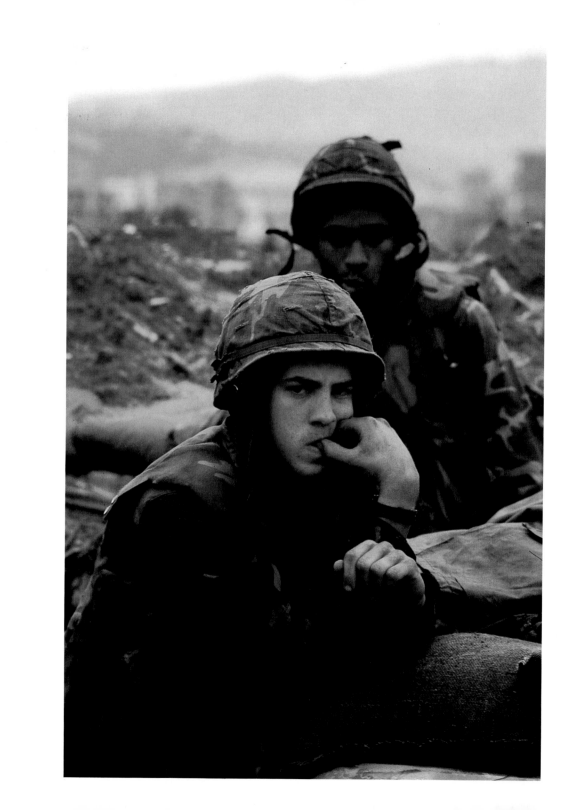

91. In the town of Suq al Gharb, a young soldier.

92. An elderly Druze in the town of Aley.

93. A model awaits her turn at the fashion show in Kaslik shopping center.

94. Palestinian fighter, Tripoli.

95. Muslim women in West Beirut.

96. At a Palestinian training camp near Tripoli.*

97. Cars passing in West Beirut.

98. A West Beirut parking lot after heavy fighting.

99. Car bombing in East Beirut.*

100. Beirut's seashore.

101. A young boy during the Shia festival of *Ashura*.*

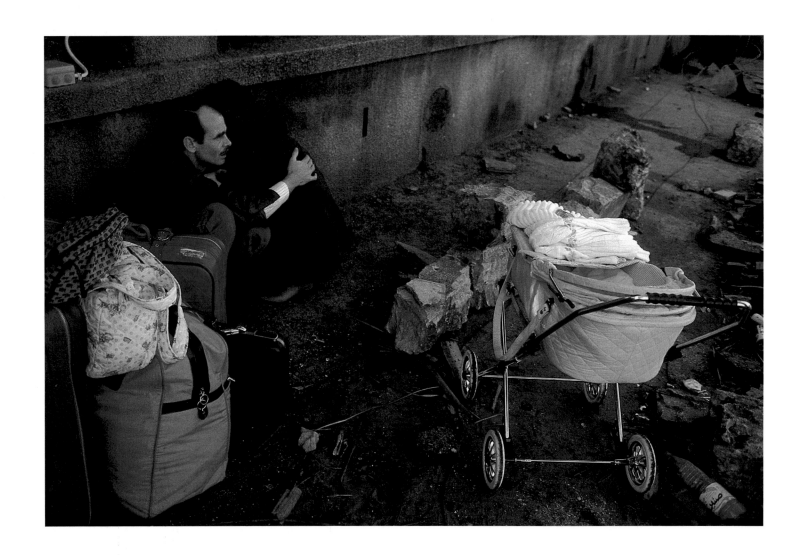

102. Avoiding sniper fire.

103. A man confronts the remains of his car.

104. Inside a mosque in the southern suburbs.

105. A Palestinian fighter in the streets of Tripoli.*

106. Beirut's Ethiopian maids on a Sunday break.

107. Hospital in Beddawi camp.

108. Rehabilitation center in East Beirut mountains.

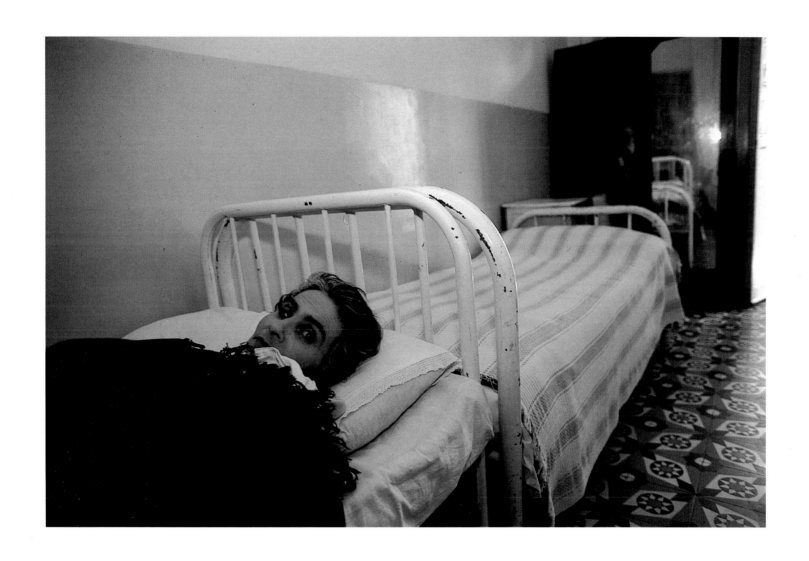

109. Asylum for the old and homeless, East Beirut.

110. Re-enacting war during shelling.

III. A rescue scene, U.S. Marine headquarters,
after the October 23, 1983, bombing.

112. A fighter's celebration in West Beirut.

113. A night out in Christian East Beirut.

114. Inside a Marine compound.

115. Street urchin in West Beirut.

116. French paratroopers mourn their comrades.

117. Fashion show in a Junieh suburb.

118. During the Palestinian fighting in Tripoli, a family leaves Tripoli hospital.

119. East Beirut supermarket.

120. Some casualties after the October 1983 attack against the U.S. Marine headquarters.

121. A scene of West Beirut.

122. On the green line in East Beirut.

123. Amal militiamen in the southern suburbs.

124. A young Palestinian boy at the front, Tripoli.

125. A Marine at his post.

126. A family, their home behind them.

127. Mountain roadside Madonna.

128. Young Shia boy during the ceremony of *Ashura*.

My Lebanon experience began in 1982 during my Nieman Fellowship year at Harvard University where I heard accounts of the 1982 Israeli invasion from visiting journalists. The stories compelled me to try to understand how the average Lebanese citizen could survive their days and nights. So I resolved to go.

When Magnum editorial director Rose Marie Wheeler casually mentioned that she wanted someone to cover both the heavy fighting in the Shuf mountains and the American marines in Beirut, I volunteered. First I telephoned Chris Steele-Perkins in London, and then paid a visit to friend Harry Mattison in New York. Both had recently returned home from Lebanon and offered me extremely useful information on how I should conduct myself in Beirut. Philip Jones Griffiths, Eugene Richards, Gille Peress, and Alex Webb also gave me good advice.

Getting to Beirut isn't easy. In late September 1983 the airport had been closed because of fighting. I flew to Larnaca, Cyprus, then boarded the Sunny Boat ferry which took me to the Christian seaport city of Junieh.

Strung unlit bulbs of the ship lights framed Junieh's early morning skyline as the ship approached port. Dawn was a soft gray slate with a tinge of pink on the horizon. I saw white smoke rising in the distance from land to the right of the direction that the ship was heading. One of the ship's crew said that it was burning garbage.

The final part of the journey involved the taking of a taxi from the Junieh seaport on the east side to the Mayflower Hotel in the Hamra district of Moslem West Beirut.

I arrived relatively wide-eyed with little historical background or perspective. I wandered around and talked to people, viewing the past through their eyes.

I had expected to live and work in Beirut no more than three weeks. Instead I stayed slightly more than four and a half months. I had little down time while I was there and I photographed everything and anyone who came near.

Beirut is a lovely place of relentlessly advancing ruin. Emergency sirens seem to be in a state of constant pain during the quiet lull after heavy shelling. The wake-up calls at one point were five-inch insects crawling over my face at 6 AM in a luxury hotel basement shelter during a twenty-hour artillery barrage. And then there were the guns of the battleship *New Jersey* firing on Druze territory, the same guns that had lulled me to sleep the previous night. Grim men ran up to barricades wearing green fatigues as formal wear or striped track suits as casual wear and carried rocket-propelled grenade launchers (RPG) as the ultimate fashion accessory.

When I arrived in Aley one morning after a night of shelling, I was taken to a hospital that had been hit by shells. The damage was severe. The chief administrator of the hospital immediately walked up to me and started screaming, "Look at what your Marines have done to my hospital." I didn't know how to respond to him. What was I going to say? This is war and Druze militias have been firing down on the Marines at the airport? That's not what he wanted to hear. His job was to heal while a soldier's job is to destroy no matter what title he is given.

A few weeks later I woke early one Sunday morning to a loud knocking on my hotel room door. My driver and friend Ali Khoury told me that there was a big explosion at the Marine base. We rushed to the scene. The date was October 23, 1983, and it *was* a big explosion.

The general feeling on the base was shock, but the Marines carried on and performed their duties with a grim purpose. Not many of them had expected the level of violence that claimed so many of their colleagues. A number of the younger Marines were not appreciative of the dangers. Up to that point it had been a beach party for many of them.

Not everyone felt that way. The French were probably not that surprised having been there with their troops for a while. A Christian Lebanese politician expressed his view on the bombing. He said that the majority of Americans are good-hearted people. He said that most Americans don't really appreciate that when their military support is sent to an area on a peace-keeping mission, there is a good chance that good men are going to die. He said that the country's leaders do understand that even if the people don't. I couldn't disagree with him as I thought of the number of innocent Lebanese citizens who were frequently killed during car bomb attacks and other violent acts of attrition by the various militias.

It was a site of madness and pain. Places where a feral alley cat and its brother rat took time from their nightly prowls to play with each other during the early hours of the evening. Where a restive formal face of tragedy attends the dying, the dead, or families in mourning.

We sit in judgment of Beirut partly as a result of the visceral image of recent kidnappings. We have here the history of five thousand years or more of living. We point in silence at the fickle finger of ethical behavior—as if we had the right. What we should do is to truly learn from it.

Two occasions of my leaving Beirut are prominent in my memory.

The first occurred while leaving Lebanon to participate in a book project in Hawaii. I had difficulty leaving because I was covering a violent internal PLO conflict in the northern port city of Tripoli and I was concerned that I was going to miss the story's conclusion. A friend urged me to leave because there was always going to be an ongoing story with or without my presence.

I remember listening to a David Bowie song from the film *The Cat People* in my airplane seat while watching the roof tops of West Beirut fall away. I listened to the song, "Putting Out Fire With Gasoline!" The lyrics captured for me certain of the terrible and tangible elements of the nature of life in Beirut. They explained the accumulated feelings I had about Lebanon after being there two months and four days.

The last time I left Beirut was May 26, 1987. I stood on the deck of the Sunny Boat as it pulled slowly out of Junieh and I watched the lights go dim. Beirut to me is a city of intense meaning, a lust for life that walks with you every day because it must. A place, borrowing a quote from a woman friend there, where "every day, every breath of fresh air must be appreciated to the fullest, because it is life."

Christian, Moslem, Druze, and Palestinian friends have all extended themselves to me during my time spent in Beirut. They did so without asking anything in return besides making an honest attempt to help me understand what is happening in their country. They wanted me to see the beauty as well as the pain. I've often thought of those moments and of my friends there. I have seen the light of Lebanon in their eyes and when it was there, it was pleasing.

Beirut Parable

Four women in covered head,
in a row,
smoking cigarettes.
One was Moslem,
one Druze,
one Palestinian,
one was Christian.
All smoking together.
Going to God in early afternoon light.
A warm friendly sun of mid autumn.
Making a prayer—full of expanding life.
Neverending—
for the waiting and the finding,
of an ultimate place in the sun.
The deepest of seas would admit the point,
a point comprised of—
ultimate good and ultimate evil.

**Equipment
Used in Beirut**

I use primarily Olympus and Leitz cameras. Olympus Cameras used were Om-1, Om-3, and Om-4 with motor drives with Olympus lenses 21mm F2, 24mm F2, 28mm F2.8, 100mm F2, 135mm F2.8, 180mm F2.8, 75 to 150mm F4, a 2x tele-extender.

Leicas used were M3, M4, M5, and M6 (motor on M6) cameras with Leitz 21mm F3.4, 28mm F2.8, 35mm F2, 50mm F2 and F1 lenses.

Canon cameras with assorted lenses were loaned to me by the Canon Camera Services department. I used Olympus cameras usually but I didn't have enough equipment at the time of my first trip. They supplied me through the kind intercession of Bruce Davidson.

I used a Minolta incident light meter for metering.

When strobes were necessary, I used a Vivitar 283 with a remote cord and a Sunpak 422. I prefer the 422 for its compact size.

I also occasionally used a compact 300mm 5.6 Celestron mirror lens, a focal length that I don't use often but felt the need to have with me on my second trip there since it was so small and light.

I used Kodak Kodrachrome 64, Ektachromes 64, 200, and tungsten 160. I exposed the Kodrachrome at 80 ASA.

Notes

10. "Martyrs'" posters in Beirut's southern suburbs.

The wall posters, the pictures of "Martyrs" who died in the civil war, have become such a prominent feature of the drawn-out war and its cult of grief and persisting violence. The young martyrs' pictures in the southern suburbs are on display right alongside the portrait of the Shia hero Imam Musa al Sadr who disappeared while on a visit to Libya's Leader Qaddafi.

11. The Maronite Patriarch, Mar Nasrallah Butrus Sufayr, and a visiting politician.

The Maronite Patriarch, Mar Nasrallah Butrus Sufayr, being visited by a politician. The Maronite Patriarch, with his seat of power in Bkerke in the heart of Maronite territory, is both a religious and political leader. The Patriarch presides over an elaborate church with vast holdings of land, with strong roots in Christian towns and villages, and in East Beirut. There is a very long tradition of politically active Patriarchs who at times challenged the power of the Maronite president and notables.

24. In the town of Suq al Gharb, a shopkeeper leaving his shop behind.

Suq al Gharb: A store owner wants to hold onto his store, a member of the Lebanese Forces tries to persuade him to flee to safety. The background to this is the tragic "battle for the mountain" between Druze and Maronites. The struggle intensified in the aftermath of Israel's invasion when units of the Maronite militia, the Lebanese Forces, emboldened by Israel's presence, spread into the ancestral home of the Druze in the Shuf mountain. After Israel opted for unilateral withdrawal in August of 1983, the position of the Maronites in the Shuf became untenable. All told, some sixty Druze–Maronite mixed villages fell to the Druze.

31. The seaside near Junieh.

Junieh, a coastal town a dozen miles north of Beirut, has emerged as the de facto capital of the Christians in Lebanon: Passage on a ship from the island of Cyprus to Junieh enables Christian travelers to avoid Beirut International Airport. The airport, on the southern approaches of Beirut, is behind Muslim lines; and besides, the intermittent rounds of fighting which shut down the airport gave the port of Junieh its chance.

46. A street in Beirut's southern suburbs.

The southern suburbs of Beirut have become a small, crowded Shia city of sorts. A quarter of a century earlier the southern approaches to the city were largely barren sand dunes. But the Shia migration from the south and the forced expulsion of the large Shia population from the northeast part of the city in 1976 brought tens of thousands of squatters and newly urbanized populations to the southern slums of Beirut. The southern alleyways are now a world unto themselves, dominated by the extremist Party of God believers and by the mainstream Shia militia, the Amal movement.

52. Maronite priest at the Maronite University of Kaslik.

The line between theology and politics blurs at the Maronite University of Kaslik—Université Saint-Esprite de Kaslik—in a Junieh suburb. Kaslik expressing the worldview of politically active and assertive priests such as Father Joseph Mouannes is a center for Maronite scholarship and advocacy. A militant group, the Maronite order of monks, has come to embody the Maronite ethos of siege and righteousness.

56. Visitors to the statue of Our Lady of Lebanon.

If there is a symbol of Christian Lebanon, Our Lady of Lebanon, or Our Lady Harissa, the guardian of Lebanon, must be as good as any. The white statue in the hills above the Bay of Junieh, with its solitude and grandeur, conveys a fitting quality of vigilance. The statue is reached by a winding road through Christian villages. Petitioners come to Our Lady Harissa for prayer, for emotional sustenance.

68. Family reunion, mountain village.

For over a decade, Lebanese have been coming and going between Beirut and their ancestral villages and towns in the hills or the hinterlands of the country, quitting the city during heavy outbursts of fighting, returning to the city when trouble trails them to their village, or when financial need makes it impossible to hold on in Beirut. This father greeting his child had just come from Beirut in one of these countless uprootings.

80. Young Shia women in Beirut's southern suburbs.

The Muslim attire of the young women is a relatively recent phenomenon: the attire isn't really "traditional." In places like Iran, Egypt, and Lebanon, and elsewhere throughout the Muslim world, the attire is both stylish and politically self-conscious, worn by young women as a statement of political and cultural identity. During the heyday of the Iranian revolution, Iranian women donned Muslim attire as a symbol of defiance against the pro-Western government of the Shah. In the southern suburbs of Beirut, the young women in this sort of attire are not passively submitting to religious tradition: the attire is worn with style and defiance.

96. At a Palestinian training camp near Tripoli.

The city of Tripoli, Lebanon's second largest city, fifty miles north of Beirut is a city of orthodox, Sunni Islam. Where Beirut looked West, Tripoli saw itself as a city of the larger entity of Syria. Trade and culture connect Tripoli to the Syrian interior. There remains to Tripoli's cultural and religious life a conservative Islamic quality that Beirut shook off long ago. Tripoli was once called *Trablus al Sham,* Tripoli of Syria, or Tripoli of Damascus. The name distinguished it from the north African city of Tripoli, Libya, and was a fair reflection of the city's identity and orientation.

99. Car bombing in East Beirut.

The car-bomb, indiscriminate in its terror and impact, aiming at civilians has by 1984–85 come to epitomize Lebanon's war. Ten years earlier it was the sniper on the rooftops of Beirut's buildings who had been the symbol of the war. Since then, the willingness to kill has reached new heights and the technological means have improved.

101. A young boy during the Shia festival of *Ashura.*

The *Ashura* celebration is the annual Shia celebration of the martyrdom of the beloved Imam Hussein, a grandson of the Prophet, in Kerbala, southern Iraq in the seventh century. These religious ceremonies arouse great enthusiasm and fervor: Men lash their bodies with chains; cut themselves with knives. *Ashura* literally means the tenth day of the Muslim month of Muharram. For nine days, there are processions of sorrow, and set pieces of lamentation for the martyred Imam and for his companions who perished with him. On the tenth day, the actual day of the Imam's martyrdom, grief reaches a fever-pitch. In towns like Nabatiye in south Lebanon as in

Iranian cities, a passion play re-enacts the siege of the saintly
Imam, how he was cut off from the water of the Euphrates by
the troops of the ruler, and how he perished with his
companions.

105. A Palestinian fighter in the streets of Tripoli.

Between 1970 and 1982, Palestinian politics in Lebanon were
for the most part played out in south Lebanon and in Beirut. In
1983 the bloodletting came to the city of Tripoli: Tripoli
became the scene of a major battle between Palestine
Liberation Organization chairman Yasser Arafat and his
Palestinian opponents sponsored by Syria. Expelled by Israel
from Beirut in the summer of 1982, Arafat returned to Tripoli
a year later, made a stand there in the Palestinian refugee
camps of Beddawi and Nahr al Barid, vowed to "fight to the
end": His forces were defeated. And on December 20, 1983,
Arafat and 4,000 of his men were evacuated by Greek ships
flying United Nations flags.

Source Notes

What follows is a brief note on sources and readings on which I relied in my writing of the text. It is not exhaustive, but there is an effort to note my indebtedness, particularly my debt to authors I did not cite directly in the text.

There is a special literary and scholarly debt that anyone writing on Lebanon, on Syria, on the Levant and its relation to the West incurs: It is a debt to the work of the distinguished Oxford historian Albert Hourani. His books and essays, written over the last four decades, are a record of the traditions and dilemmas of the eastern Arabs—the Lebanese included—since their encounter with the West in the late eighteenth century. His books, *Arabic Thought in the Liberal Age* (London: Oxford University Press, 1970), *Syria and Lebanon* (London: Oxford University Press, 1946), and *Minorities in the Arab World* (London: Oxford University Press, 1947) are outstanding works.

The title "The City of Regrets" was suggested by an essay of Jan Morris on Beirut, "The Impossible City," in her book of travel *Among the Cities* (New York: Oxford University Press, 1985).

One of the historians of the Phoenicians is Gerhard Hern, *The Phoenicians* (New York: Morrow, 1975).

The Egyptian background to the Druze story, including the description of Al Hakim, is told by Marshall G. S. Hodgson, *The Venture of Islam*, Vol. 2 (Chicago and London: University of Chicago Press, 1974). The narrative on the Druze is drawn from Charles H. Churchill's two books, *Mount Lebanon: A Ten Year Residence from 1842 to 1852* (London: Saunders and Otley, 1853), and *The Druzes and the Maronites Under Turkish Rule* (London: Spottiswoods, 1862.)

The section on the Maronites relies on an essay by the leading contemporary historian of the Maronites, Kamal Salibi, "The Maronite Experience," *Middle East Insight*, Vol. V, No. 1 (1987).

C. F. Volney's remarkable book of travel is *Travels Through Egypt and Syria* (New York: John Tiobout, 1798).

Napoleon Bonaparte's Egyptian adventure is told by many historians. Barbara Tuchman's *Bible and Sword* (New York: Ballantine, 1984) is one source; E. M. Forster, *Alexandria: A History and a Guide* (New York: Oxford University Press, 1986 edition) tells that story with great artistry.

The best history of nineteenth-century Beirut is Leila Tarazi Fawaz, *Merchants and Migrants in Nineteenth Century Beirut* (Cambridge: Harvard University Press, 1983). There is a great photographic record, using old postcards, and a beautiful text on the "old town" of Beirut by Fouad Debbas, *Beirut: Our Memory* (Beirut: Naufal Group, 1986).

The debate about "smaller" and Greater Lebanon, including some of the diplomatic memoranda of the time, can be found in Meir Zamir, "Smaller and Greater Lebanon—The Squaring of a Circle?" *The Jerusalem Quarterly* (Spring 1982).

The making of the National Pact of 1943 is drawn from the Ph.D. dissertation of a young Lebanese scholar, Farid el-Khazen, *The Disintegration of the Lebanese Confessional System* (Baltimore: Johns Hopkins University, 1986).

The Palestinian interlude in Lebanon has been recounted by the Palestinian scholar and historian Walid Khalidi, *Conflict and Violence in Lebanon* (Cambridge: Harvard Studies in International Affairs, 1979). The political memoir of Abu Iyad cited in the text is *My Home, My land* (New York: Times Books, 1978).

A sociological portrait of Beirut before and after its collapse has been drawn by the Lebanese sociologist Samir Khalaf, *Lebanon's Predicament* (New York: Columbia University Press, 1987).

Joseph Chami, a Lebanese journalist, has pieced together, in photo and text, the story of the first eighteen months of war in *Days of Tragedy—Lebanon 75–76* (Beirut: private printing, 1977).

The background to and the course of Israel in Lebanon is

told by Ze'ev Schiff and Ehud Ya'ari in *Israel's Lebanon War*
(New York: Simon and Schuster, 1984), and Jonathan Randal,
Going All the Way (New York: Vintage, 1984).

The story of the U.S. Marines in Lebanon was covered by
Eric Hammel in *The Root* (San Diego, New York, and London:
Harcourt Brace Jovanovich, 1985).

Malcolm Kerr's 1981 essay on Arab politics cited in the text
is "Rich and Poor in the Arab Order," *Journal of Arab Affairs*,
Vol. 1, No. 1 (October 1981).

The political phenomenon of Shia power in Lebanon is the
subject of Augustus Richard Norton, *Amal and the Shia*
(Austin: University of Texas Press, 1987).

Farid el Khazen's letter from Beirut appeared in *The
Washington Post*, June 2, 1987. The essay was aptly entitled
"The Killing Field of the Middle East."

Index

Plate numbers appear in *italics*.

"Abu Abdu the Kurd," 46
Adonis, 36–37
Alawi sect, 11
Aley, *39, 49, 92*
Amal militia, 44–45
American University of Beirut, 10, 24, 27, 41–42
Arab-Israeli conflict, 9–10, 28, 30, 31, 36, 42, 43
Arab Tells His Story, An (Atiyah), 18
Arafat, Yasser, 29, 30, 47, *182*
Ashura, 181, 101, 128
Assad, Hafez, 33–34, 44
Atiyah, Edward, 18

Beddawi refugee camp, *182, 4, 7, 18, 23, 35, 47, 60, 88, 107*
Begin, Menachem, 28, 35, 36, 38
Beirut:
    American embassy bombing in (1983), 41
    Armenian-Shia neighborhood of, 23
    Ashrafieh quarter of, 23–24
    assimilation in, 10, 17, 23, 38
    Basta quarter of, 24
    "belt of misery" around, 27, 30
    Cairo compared with, 10–11, 25
    as capital, 18–19
    car bombings in, *181, 99, 103*
    cease-fires in, 9
    Christianity vs. Islam in, 10, 17–18, 19–20, 24, 26, 27, 32, 35
    Damascus compared with, 11, 17, 25, 34
    demographic balance in, 17–18, 30–31
    descriptions of, 16–17, 23–24, 25–26, 34–35, 47
    destruction of, 9–10, 34–35, 47
    East, 24, 45, 181, *6, 15, 29, 34, 40, 51, 71, 77, 81, 99, 113, 119, 122*
    European influence on, 17
    fashion in, 33, 46
    French influence on, 9, 24
    French troops in, 41, 177, *116*
    graffiti in, 33
    "green line" in, 10, *19, 65, 122*
    homeless in, *109*
    Hooterville neighborhood of, 40, 41
    hostage-taking in, 9, 46
    Israeli seige of, 36–38
    Karantina area of, 32
    massacres in, 32–33, 38–39
    multinational force in, 38, 39, 40
    Muslim vs. Western culture in, 9, 10, 17, 24, 25
    myths of, 10
    natural beauty of, 18
    "old town" of, 23
    Palestinian control of, 10, 23, 32
    Palestinians evacuated from, 38, *182*
    as parody, 9
    as "permissive" environment, 40
    pillage of, 34
    port of, 17, *100*
    prostitution in, *17, 63*
    Ras Beirut area of, 24
    shantytowns of, 27, 30
    Shia neighborhoods of, 10, 22–23, 32
    al Shuwayfat suburb of, *20*
    snipers in, *103*
    souks of, 23
    southern suburbs of, 180, *21, 25, 46, 48, 58, 80, 85, 104, 123*
    Street urchins in, *115*
    Sunni neighborhoods in, 24
    Syrian occupation of, 47
    as trading center, 11–12, 16, 17
    "turfs" in, 32–33, 43–44
    U.S. Marines in, 10, 26–27, 40–41, 177–78, *26, 43, 61, 69, 73, 75, 90, 111, 114, 120, 125*
    U.S. occupation of, 24, 39–43
    "war of the camps" in, 47
    West, 35, 39, 42, 44, 45, 47, 177, *30, 33, 41, 62, 76, 82, 83, 84, 95, 97, 98, 112, 115, 121*
"Beirut Parable," 178
Beirut: '75 (Samman), 31–32
Bekaa Valley, 9, 22, 27, 43
Bowie, David, 178
Byzantine Empire, 14

Cat People, The, 178
Central Intelligence Agency (CIA), 9
Chami, Joseph, 34
Chamoun, Camille, 26, 27, 31, 33
Chiha, Michel, 20, 27
Conrad, Joseph, 41
Couget, Joseph, 46
"cowboy, the," 46
Crusades, 14–15

Damur Brigade, 32
Damur massacre, 32, 33
Darazi, Muhammad Ibn Ismail al, 13
"Desert, The" (Adonis), 36–37
Druze:
    dissimulation in, 13–14
    hereditary privilege in, 13
    Maronites vs., 12, 13, 15, 18, 19–20,
        29–30, 31, 41
    origins of, 13–14, 5
    as political faction, 12, 13–14, 31, 40,
        41, 42, 44
Dulles, John Foster, 26
Durrell, Lawrence, 25
Egypt:
    Nasser's rule of, 24, 25, 26, 28, 36
    Western influence on, 10–11
Eisenhower Doctrine, 26
Ethiopians, 16, 106

Fatah, 32, 33
Fawaz, Leila Tarazi, 17
Francis I, King of France, 15
Friedman, Thomas, 40, 41

Gemayyel, Amin, 39, 40, 1
Gemayyel, Basheer, 38–39, 44
Gibran, Kahlil, 12
Goodell, William, 16–17
Greek Orthodox church, 16, 18
Griffiths, Philip Jones, 177

Haddad, Saad, 46
Hakim, al–, 13
Halloum, Ali, 40

Hammel, Eric, 40–41
Hashemite monarchy, 26
Heart of Darkness (Conrad), 41
Homer, 11
hostages, 9, 46
Hourani, Albert, 25
"hunters of foreigners," 9
Hussein Ibn Talal, King of Jordan, 28
Hussein, Imam, 22, 181

Imarah, 13
Innocents Abroad (Twain), 17
Iraq, 26
Islam:
    Alawi, 11
    Arab nationalism and, 22
    Christianity vs., 10, 17–18, 19–20, 24,
        26, 27, 32, 35
    Druze sect in, 13–14
    fundamentalist, 45–46
    Ismaili, 13
    Shia, 13, 45–46
    Sunni, 11, 45
    women and, 181, 80
Ismaili sect, 13
Israel:
    Lebanon invaded by, 10, 28, 35–39,
        46–47, 180
    wars fought by, 9–10, 28, 30, 31, 36,
        42, 43

Jordan, 28
Junblatt, Kamal, 14, 29, 34
Junieh, 177, 180, 2, 3, 13, 31, 42, 72, 77,
    79, 117

Kahan, Yitzhak, 39
Kahan Commission of Inquiry, 39
Kalashnikov rifle, 33
Kaslik shopping center, 93
Kerr, Malcolm, 41–42
Kerr, Stanley, 42
Khalaf, Salah, 30
Khomeini, Ayatollah Ruhollah, 31, 41,
    45, 46
Khoury, Ali, 177
Khuri, Bishara al, 21

Lady Harissa (Our Lady of Lebanon),
    181, 27, 56
Lahd, Antoine, 46
Land and the Book, The (Thomson), 17
Lawrence, T.E., 9
Lebanese Armed Forces, 40, 180, 14,
    74
Lebanese National Movement, 31
Lebanon:
    Arab-Israeli conflict and, 9–10, 28,
        30, 31, 36, 42, 43
    Arab nationalism and, 24–25, 26,
        29–30, 33, 45–46
    census of (1932), 30–31
    civil war in (1958), 34
    communal war in (1860), 15
    compromise in, 21
    constitution of, 21
    Druze faction in, 12, 13–14, 31, 40,
        41, 42, 44
    Druze vs. Maronite factions in, 12,
        13, 15, 18, 19–20, 29–30, 31, 41
    formation of, 12–13, 16, 18–20

"Free," 46–47

freedom of press in, 27–28

French mandate over, 12, 14–16, 19–20, 21

as "garden without fences," 9

"Greater," 16, 18–20

Greek Orthodox faction in, 18

hybrid culture in, 12

ideological void in, 28, 29

inequalities in, 27

internal conflict in, 28–30, 31–32

Iran and, 22

Israeli invasion of, 10, 28, 35–39, 46–47, 180

"Lebanonism" vs. Pan-Arabism in, 29–30

Maronite faction in, 12, 13, 14–15, 21, 22, 31, 32, 39, 41, 42, 44

as Mediterranean country, 20

militias and private armies in, 30, 31, 44

"mountain" vs. "sea" in, 11–12, 13, 20

myths about, 11–13, 20

National Pact for, 21

oil industry and, 25, 30, 42

Palestinian army in, 28–29, 30, 31, 32, 34, 35–36, 38–39, 182, 28

Palestinian refugee camps in, 9–10, 25, 28–29, 47

peasants vs. traders in, 15, 17

Phoenician origins of, 11–12, 19, 20

as playground of wealthy, 25

political character of, 20–22, 25, 26, 27–28, 40

political factions in, 12–13, 20–22, 27, 44

polyglot culture of, 25

press coverage of, 25, 26, 40

as republic, 18–21, 24, 27–28

security zone in, 46–47

Shia faction in, 12, 20, 21, 22–23, 29, 31, 40, 41, 42, 43, 44, 47, 180, 181

silk industry of, 15, 16, 19

Six Day War (1967) and, 28

South, 38, 46–47

Sunni faction in, 12, 18, 20, 21–22, 23, 29, 31, 181

Syria and, 19, 21

Syrian occupations of, 10, 33–34, 35, 36, 44, 47

U.S. influence on, 10, 26

U.S. naval bombardment of, 41, 43, 177, 49

villages in, 18, 23, 45, 68

see also Beirut

"Lebanonism," 29–30

Leo X, Pope, 15

"Little Lebanon is Cosmopolitan," 26–27

Louis IX (Saint Louis), King of France, 14

Marines, U.S., 10, 26–27, 40–41, 177–78, 26, 43, 61, 69, 73, 75, 90, 111, 114, 120, 125

Maron, John, 14

Maronites:

  as Christians, 14–15, 180

  Druze vs., 12, 13, 15, 18, 19–20, 29–30, 31, 41

  Israeli aid to, 35–36

  militias of, 32, 33, 35, 40, 44, 37

  origins of, 14–15

  Palestinians vs., 35, 44

  Party of God vs., 45

  Patriarch of, 14, 180, 11

  as political faction, 12, 13, 14–15, 21, 22, 31, 32, 39, 41, 42, 44

  Syrian aid to, 33–34, 35, 44

  U.S. aid to, 40

Maronite University of Kaslik, 180, 52

"martyrs" posters, 10

Marun, Yuhanna, 14

Mattison, Harry, 177

Merchants and Migrants in Nineteenth Century Beirut (Fawaz), 17

Miss Lebanon, 64

Morris, Jan, 25–26

Mouannes, Joseph, 180

Mount Lebanon, 16, 27

Muhammad, 22

Muharram, 181

Na'aman, Boulos, 33

Nabatiye, 9

Nahar, An, 31, 40

Nahr al Barid refugee camp, 182, 50, 53

Napoleon I, Emperor of France, 15–16

Napoleon III, Emperor of France, 15–16

Nasser, Gamal Abdul, 24, 25, 26, 28, 36

New Jersey, 177

New York Times, 26–27

"occultation," 22
October War (1973), 36
Ottoman Empire, 12, 13, 16, 19, 23
Our Lady of Lebanon (Lady Harissa),
    181, *27, 56*

Palestine Liberation Organization, 10,
    32, 35, 36, 39, 178
    Arafat's leadership of, 29, 30, 47, 182
Palestinians:
    in Beirut, 10, 23, 32, 38, 182
    Maronites vs., 35, 44
    Phalangist massacre of, 38–39
    as political faction, 28–29, 30, 31, 32,
        34, 35–36, 38–39, 182
    refugee camps of, 9–10, 25, 28–29,
        47, *32, 86*
    in Tripoli, *22, 38, 87, 94, 96, 105,
        118, 124*
Party of God, 44, 45, 46, 47, 180
Peress, Gille, 177
Phalange, 31, 38–39, 40–41
Phoenicia, 11–12, 19, 20
Protestants, 18
"Putting Out the Fire With Gasoline!"
    (Bowie), 178

Qabbani, Nizzar, 47
Qaddafi, Muamar al, 36, 43, 180

Ramadan, 24
Reagan, Ronald, 36, 38
Reagan Administration, 42
rehabilitation centers, *81, 108*
Richards, Eugene, 177
rocket-propelled grenade launchers
    (RPG), 177
Root, The (Hammel), 40–41

Sabra and Shatila refugee camps, *32, 86*
Sadat, Anwar el, 10–11
Sadr, Musa al, 31, 43, 44
Said, Ali Ahmad, 36–37
"Saif al Dahia," 46
Saint Joseph University, 27
Samman, Ghada al, 31
Sharon, Ariel, 28, 35, 36
Shia faction:
    neighborhoods of, 10, 22–23, 32, 67,
        123
    as political organization, 12, 20, 21,
        22–23, 29, 31, 40, 41, 42, 43,
        44, 47, 180, 181, *8*
    as religious sect, 13, 45–46, *78*
Sidon, 16
Six Day War (1967), 28
Solh, Riad al, 21
South Lebanon Army, 46
Steele-Perkins, Chris, 177
Sufayr, Mar Nasrallah Butrus, 180, *11*

Sunni faction:
    neighborhoods of, 24
    as political organization, 12, 18, 20,
        21–22, 23, 29, 31, 181
    as religious sect, 11, 45
Suq al Gharb, 180, *24, 89, 91*

Taqiyya, 13–14
Tel Zaatar siege, 32–33
terrorism, 41
Thomson, W.M., 17
Tigers, 31, 33
Tripoli, 16, 19, 181, *12, 22, 38, 54, 55,
    70, 87, 94, 96, 105, 118, 124*
Tueni, Ghassan, 40
Twain, Mark, 17

Umma, 45
United Nations, 25
University of Kaslik, 33

Versailles Peace Conference, 19
Volney, C.F. de, 15

Webb, Alex, 177
Wheeler, Rose Marie, 177
William of Tyre, 14

Zionism, 35